THE H[AT MAN]

THE TRUE STORY OF EVIL ENCOUNTERS

HEIDI HOLLIS

Level Head Publishing

www.levelheadpublishing.com

OTHER BOOKS BY HEIDI HOLLIS

ADULT BOOKS:

The Other "F" Word:
A Book on Faith in the Real (Funny) World

Jesus Is No Joke:
A True Story of an Unlikely Witness Who Saw Jesus

The Secret War:
A True Story About A Real Alien War and Shadow
People

How to Pray Like the Angels:
A True Story About Picture Prayers

KIDS BOOKS:

Diary Blog of the Fickle Finders:
Investigates—The Other "F" Word

Diary Blog of the Fickle Finders:
Investigates—Angels or Heroes

www.HeidiHollis.com

The Hat Man: The True Story of Evil Encounters
Copyright 2014 by Heidi Hollis
July 2014

Level Head Publishing books may be ordered at discount rates when purchased in quantity for premiums and promotions, as well as, for educational and fundraising uses. Special editions can also be made for events.
For details, contact: levelheadpub@gmail.com

Photos are published by arrangement with the author and photographer
Cover design by Heidi Hollis

Author Note: I have tried to recreate events, locales and conversations from my memories of them. In order to maintain their anonymity in some instances I have changed the names of individuals and places, I may have changed some identifying characteristics and details such as physical properties, gender, occupations and places of residence.

Level Head Publishing books may be ordered through booksellers or by contacting:
Level Head Publishing, LLC
Milwaukee, WI 53224

www.levelheadpublishing.com
levelheadpub@gmail.com

(EBook) ISBN 978-0-9830401-5-6
(Soft Cover) ISBN 978-0-9830401-9-4

Dedicated to winning the
battle of ALL battles.

&

Inspired by ALL who do right by God,
And for those who aspire to one day.

TABLE OF CONTENTS

INTRODUCTION:

What You Hold In Your Hands

For those of you unfamiliar with my work and writings, one could say that I take an unlikely approach when it comes to the paranormal and otherworldly mysteries. I say it's "unlikely," because I don't always keep a straight face when relaying strange things. For some people, that spells that I don't take these topics as seriously as needed. However, I do take these topics highly seriously. I just don't see the point to always keeping things fully creepy in order to relay what is—to me—just another reality mixed into this life.

I feel if we are ever to have a true understanding about paranormal mysteries then we need to delve into these topics as we would any other topic—as humanly as possible. That means we attack it head-on, fully flawed, wrinkled foreheads in wonder, and with a smile awkwardly strewn across our faces. This is the way of our forefathers and this is the only way I personally feel works best.

If I ever want to clear a room or have people request I change the subject so they will be able to sleep at night, all I have to do is share a few of the thousands of stories sent my way of paranormal horror. But if I want to hear thoughtful questions, see inspired raises of the eyebrow—all I have to do is be myself when presenting these paranormally charged topics where I can laugh if I want, show disappointment, despair, outrage and hope for answers to the topic at hand.

So here's to hoping that a new era in discussing and discovering answers to the paranormal world are unfolded and presented with a gleam in our eyes, a light in our minds and answers falling off our lips and unto pages. This book is a look into my life and world intertwined with the paranormal and how I came across a phenomenon, researched it and somehow gave it a name that has stuck till this day—**"The Hat Man."**

1

TASTES LIKE CHICKEN:

My Beef And Background

I adore my sanity as much as the next person. It's not an easy task to hold on to at times when being met by some of the things that I have and that most people deem to be only science fiction. As with anyone, I have my likes and dislikes, favorites and unfamiliar prospects that don't interest me. I like indulging in special effect-driven movies, rollerblading, traveling abroad to different countries when possible, dishing out special patience to my dear patients as a practicing occupational therapist and laughing to no end at most things in life.

I'm a colorful, boring, lighthearted, fearful, and caring individual. I have failures and dreams, procrastination and domination, laughter and breakdowns—all rolled up into my wicked little rock I call my life. No one has this thing to live but me and if anyone knows any better, they wouldn't want to borrow my shoes for a night on the town!

The world of the paranormal lives in my shoes. It has at times danced around the laces, untied them to trip me up, and other times dug deep between my toes to make them dance to a different tune than others. It's been an interesting life to say the least, thus far. Then, just when I thought God could show me no more, another page of strange smells floats my way.

Neat imagery, huh? I'm good for it, just wait it gets better. ☺

I always like to give a little background on who I am and where the heck I'm coming from so people get a good look at "those people" who deal with the paranormal.

I have been living in the nest of the paranormal world for nearly as long as I can recall. Starting at the age of seven, I lived in a haunted house and I wish that's all I had to say about that, but it isn't.

When I say "haunted," I'm saying that all of the scary movies ever put out about ghosts and hauntings were therapeutic for myself and my siblings while growing up. It was like comfort food for us to know that even if the stories we were seeing weren't true, at least we knew others had an idea of the possibilities out there. With flying silverware, organs playing by themselves, loud poundings being heard, attic doors falling open, spirits being photographed, red-eyed-black birds attacking indoors—one could surmise that the possibilities were absolutely terrifying for us.

We didn't enjoy what was happening to us in the least, but it got me and my siblings' interest to watch even more horrifying depictions of scary things on television and in movies. If you have ever been home alone, but thought you weren't and heard a suspicious noise and went to investigate it while calling out your sister's name only to find it wasn't your sister—then you can join my private corner in memories of hell breaking loose! Allow me to share:

I had to be around the ripe age of nine when I came home from school to meet my sister at the front door. It was a known rule with my siblings and I, that even if our dad didn't admit (at the time—although he confessed later) that the house was haunted, we would watch each other's back so none of us would be home alone. So, my older sister always sat on the front porch of our house to wait for me to come home from school.

On this developing crappy day, my sister wasn't standing on the front porch, so I assumed she had to go inside for a good reason. So in the house I go, calling out my sister's name when I hear a sound coming from the kitchen. It sounded like silverware clanging together, so I figured she must have gotten hungry while waiting for me and went in to make herself something to eat.

"Wow! She's brave!" I thought her to be at the moment.

Once through the front door I headed through the living room, passing the first floor bathroom in the direction of the kitchen. Along the way, I tossed down my book bag and continued to call out my sister's name. As I rounded the corner towards the kitchen, I remember having my head down while fumbling to unzip my jacket. Then I looked up to see why my sister wasn't answering me and why the sounds of silverware clanging seemed to be just that—with no end!

Glancing up, I didn't see my sister in the kitchen.

I looked around the corner to my left (inside of the kitchen), and then looked in the direction of the silverware sounds. It was coming from *inside* of the kitchen drawer and it grew louder as I stood there! The thoughts that raced through my mind at what it could be made my body go into uncontrollable shudders.

I know a stressed look must have come across my face as I looked towards the drawer and watched as it began to shake from the rattling silverware housed on the inside! That look must have quickly turned to one of terror as I watched the drawer slide open, on its own will, to reveal silverware rising up into the air. My curiosity about the whole situation was immediately cured—if there were any questions left in me at all!

I didn't stick around to see where that silverware decided to go next, all I felt is that a target may have just been painted on my forehead—so I simply bolted! I spun around and out of the kitchen I went heading for the nearest sense of security I could think of—the bathroom! It had a door to it and a lock, so that spelled out quick protection of some sort to this nine-year-old kid.

As I lunged for the bathroom door I thought it was odd that it was closed tightly, although apparently no one was home. I reached for the doorknob and quickly tried to turn it—but the door was locked! Had my sister already been met with the silverware party or had a sneaky fork already planned ahead of what my next move would be and locked the door?!

No time to think, I had to get to the other choice of security—the second floor bathroom!

The staircase stood right before me as I spun away from the locked door and leapt up the stairs like no other! Then down the hall and into the bathroom I went, locked the door and stepped away from it. There was no putting my back against the door and slipping down to try to hear anything coming where I might get a free ear piercing through the door! Nope! Instead, I fully backed away to the opposite wall and waited.

There's no telling how many moments passed before I heard what sounded like silverware clicking together in the air outside of the door. Several taps and scrapings of what sounded like silverware going against the door were clearly heard, but there was no getting me any closer than that to verify anything. I was standing stiff as a board, staring in question and in terror as I listened to evil coming for me!

As the clanging sounds intermittently came and went, tears came as I finally sat down and waited to be rescued from the horror I was enduring. I wasn't sure what had happened to my sister, even if she was okay or not. The worries that paralyzed me and blurred my thoughts were devastating and it seemed I was trapped in that position to no end. I thought about what I would do if whatever it was outside the door, decided to turn the lock to open the door where their access would be unlimited.

"What would I see if the door opened? What would it do to me? How many hands did it have to be able to toss around that much silverware and why was it doing this to me?" I couldn't help but to wonder.

I buried my face into my bent knees to help calm myself and absorb my tears. I don't know how much time had passed when I finally heard something louder than the silverware sounds! A door had opened up, but it wasn't to the bathroom—thank God! I then heard cries from my dad calling out my name, but I couldn't move.

Was I hearing things, was something playing tricks on me? The mental torture I had just endured made me question reality to every extent. I sat and listened some more, then I heard footsteps coming up the stairway.

A loud knock came to the door, "Heidi, are you in there?" My dad shouted. I breathed for what felt like the first time during the whole ordeal, but I still could hardly move as I quietly answered my dad. Numb legs still in tote, I stood up and cautiously opened the door. It was indeed my daddy!

He asked why I didn't answer or come downstairs when he first called out to me. As I stood in the doorway of the bathroom, I managed to I recant my horror story to him into his doubtful eyes. Then to my added horror and proof, there laid a spoon on the floor next to the bathroom door! Yes, it was only a single spoon, but a spoon indeed and not quite in a place commonly found. It was all still of no relevance for my dad and stepmom where I was discounted as being any sort of reliable witness—just merely a scared nine year old.

I later learned that my sister didn't come home after school that day because of a school function, my parents had regrettably forgotten about it. My parent's disbelief about the incident sounds like a typical scenario for children who experience the paranormal, but I at least had the comfort of my siblings who all had their own personal encounters where they could fully relate to my own.

So there goes my "Attack of the Killer Spoon" story and it wasn't the first, or last odd thing to happen to me in this spooky life. We moved from that haunted home and into a newly built home, slightly due to some encouragement to live in a home with no history attached to it. It was a refreshing new start to go from the city to the outskirts of town where relocating turtles, minnows and snakes into my parent's new bathtub was my focal point. It wasn't much appreciated by my folks for some reason, but my younger sister and I felt it added life to the place!

We no longer had any spectral visitors stop by to harass any of us anymore, but there were peculiar instances that still took place. My two sisters and I weren't always the full "buddy-buddy" types—we definitely had our squabbles.

Yet, we had something very much in common that we were unaware of for years.

My mother passed away when I was seven years old, it was shortly after that when the haunting began in our old home. I don't believe my mother was responsible for the haunting directly, because it simply wouldn't make sense that she would take aim at her own young children to terrorize them. But I do believe when she lived, that her presence kept whatever darkness was in the home at a distance to stay away from us. When she died, it seems the darkness was able to creep in freely.

Soon after moving into our newly built home, though, my dreams started to change...

I had some wonderful dreams where I saw white robed people guiding me and teaching me various elements I knew to be spiritually evolved. I just couldn't ever fully recall all of those elements. But, I was left more with a sense of a deep knowing and understanding of how to access what was taught. That when I needed the information that was imprinted on me, that is when it would come forward in my mind. This place where I was taught these insights was an unbelievable place to be. The buildings looked very much like the ancient buildings of Greece, but made of sparkling and nearly see-through crystals. So I always referred to it as the "Crystal City" and the buildings I was taught at there, I deemed to be "schools."

As a child, I found these so-called "dreams" to be inspiring and nothing I could or would keep quiet about—so I shared it with my younger sister openly. My visits to this Crystal City continued throughout my life and they seemed so very real that I called them "waking dreams." I was shocked later in life to find others who also claimed to have visited this place in their dreams, even where some outright drew and described the exact buildings I recalled.

Had my dreams and eyes only been filled with holy visions and inspirations, this might be a short book. My sisters and I weren't lucky enough to share visions of this beautiful place. Instead, we found we had another set of journey's that were separate, dark and undefined.

As my dreams turned into visions of light and knowledge, my mother started appearing in my dreams—but she wasn't the person I knew her to be. These dreams were dark, scary and absolutely to the core of creepiness! There was no warmth, no love, and no light in these dreams. She was not herself, and these images were not her.

Something liked to take the form of my mother, tricking me to come closer to greet her, only for this image of her to attack and send me running, scared and confused! There was always a supernatural element in these dreams and such a sense of evil that was not humanly possible. These were the dreams I shared with my siblings, unfortunately.

None of us were very forthcoming to admit that images of our dearly missed mother were coming to us in the form of something demonic. It was disturbing and intruded upon our lives where we each lost sleep over it and contemplated on our own as to what was taking place and why. After years of this, my older sister had just moved out of the house when she called one day and told me how she wasn't able to sleep. She told me that she was having horrid dreams about our mom attacking her and that it just made no sense why these dreams kept coming up. I was stunned and then told her that I was having similar dreams and so was our younger sister. None of our dreams were exactly the same, though close, but they all had a similar theme where they weighed on our minds.

These scenarios lasted for years, well into my 20's, and they will forever live on in my memory. When others I loved have passed away, I always got a pleasant visit afterwards via a dream or sense of them being near. That never happened with my mother and psychic friends volunteered to tell me different reasons why that was. Some said that my mother had already reincarnated, or that she was watching over me as my guardian angel so they couldn't understand why I didn't sense her being so near to me already.

All I knew was that my mom's image was used to create horror in my dreams. I also knew that just because she was my mom, didn't mean that she wasn't without her flaws. Speaking honestly; there was no telling what may have become of her—we can't *all* go to Heaven—can we?

So, one can imagine that I wasn't fully receptive when a psychic friend of mine came on my radio show, *Heidi Hollis-The Outlander*, and she wanted to connect me with my mom's soul. I insisted that wasn't necessary and I did my best to divert the topic. A few things got said about my mom and it gladly was brief. After the show, I shared with my psychic friend of the demonic form my mother came as for years, attacking myself and my siblings.

Innocently, my psychic friend focuses on "love and light" in all that she sees, which is a gift I wish I could filter to only show that side, too. But, that sadly isn't my reality. My friend insisted that my mother isn't a demon and that my mom expressed to her how proud she is of me. I was silent about these revelations, because they didn't seem like the "mom" who had been visiting me. However, I did agree that I didn't think my mom is necessarily a demon—that's a horrible thought that anyone might be at any point in the afterlife.

Well, my perception of this "dream demon mom" was about to be reaffirmed!

The next day after my show, I got an explosive email from my psychic friend who told of her daughter waking up in the middle of the night—screaming that she was being attacked by a "demon woman" with black eyes! My friend calmed her daughter down and said she had never had her daughter have such an encounter before. My friend returned to her bedroom, only to be met by the same demon woman who physically attacked her—pinning her down on the bed!!!

To make a long story short, I confirmed in a nutshell to my friend in silly sarcasm, "Wow! Now *that* sounds like my mom! Wow! You really *were* in touch with her!" This of course wasn't the "proud of you" mom she mentioned to be in touch with earlier. There was no "love and light" floating around with this demon mama!

I couldn't help but to feel bad that this demonic thing had attacked my friend and her daughter, of course. I sort of felt like apologizing about it happening, as if I were somehow responsible. Then another realization hit me in knowing that this dark entity was *so* close and *still* listening after all of these years! That was highly disturbing to know that evil ears were near!

Yet, it was kind of fun and funny when I recounted the story to my family about what took place. We all concurred that it indeed sounded to be exactly the "dream mom" showing its true dark colors. We are kind of used to this sort of thing and we know what we know, no matter how good someone else's psychic perception is. Trusting one's own gut surpasses anyone else's beliefs, though their intentions may be fully pure.

One thing those "mom dreams" had in common with the more spiritually positive ones is that they both seemed *so* real that both dream types changed my perception on this world. Growing up in the new house also brought astral trips where I flew over buildings, woke up next to something cold against my cheek only to see it was the ceiling of my bedroom and I experienced a variety of what would seem to be like prophetic dreams.

At one point, as a teenager, I started to see strange lights in the skies. They were nothing phenomenally cool—just odd. I worked at a local McDonald's and often walked or biked home, even when heaps of snow tried to blanket me to my death during the rough, Wisconsin Winters. So my walks from work were often at night and I lived away from any major city lights that could occlude my seeing the night sky.

Mainly what I saw then were very high, bright lights that either seemed to linger too long, or move too quickly. I truly didn't know what to think of it, but I had my suspicions these were otherworldly bits I got a glimpse of. Then came my bumping into an interesting book that I knew I had to have that just so happened to deal with the alien abduction phenomena being reported. I was still a kid at the time, when quickly my interests in ghostly phenomena got accompanied with the aliens abound.

As an adult, strangeness continued to follow me. The notion inside of me that existed there since I was a child, also grew louder exclaiming that something was different about me and that it was time that I found some answers. As my interests in the world of the strange continued to grow, so did my inner me and my personal views of this world and others.

I started to have the unfortunate "gift" of seeing dead people, or some kind of people. I really didn't have much interest to see any ghosts. Heck! I'd lived with ghosts before and I really didn't feel they had much to offer me but headaches and horror!

In fact, I was way too chicken to poke around looking for ghosts. I was already afraid of the dark (when I became a teenager this fear started), simply because I knew what the darkness had to hide and they could keep hiding for all I cared!

I can't say I was some kind of seer who could spot out any ghost or spirit I wanted, either, because I didn't want to! If I saw something not alive as we know it, you can bet Heidi was trying to look the other way or shoo it away!

It always was an accidental encounter when I happened to pay attention to a ghost, because *they* popped up, not the other way around. In fact, one of my last major run-ins with a ghost was several years back. Okay I need to be fully honest here; I do still see these things, but nothing that has been quite as disruptive as this incidence:

Sometime in the Fall of 2004, I had a pretty exhausting day, so when it came time to go to sleep that night that was all I wanted to do. So, I was sound asleep when I suddenly felt a presence in my bedroom. Fortunately and unfortunately, I'm one of those people who pops right up when something out-of-the-ordinary stops by. Whether it's good or bad, there's just some instinct that says, "Here we go, Heidi!" Then I go!

So of course, I prop myself up in bed to have a look and right next to me on my left, is a woman, all-aglow! There was a light from a streetlight entering my room, but this woman also seemed to have a light emitting from her that only lit her up. This woman was dressed in what appeared to be a white dress, maybe slightly grey in color that was gathered in the middle by a cloth of some kind. It appeared to be very old fashioned, dated by some time period I wasn't aware of. She was short in stature, just under five feet tall, a bit heavyset and she's standing maybe two to three feet from me!

At this point, I had just woke up and opened my eyes to see this very solid looking woman standing next to my bed when she starts to reach for me. When I say solid, she was not wispy, see-through or any of that. She was standing on her own two feet on the floor with an arm outstretched my way with long-puffy sleeves! One would think that I might hurdle myself out of her way and scream—right? But on this particular night I was *really* tired! I hadn't been sleeping for long when in pops this lady to wake me to her presence, so I was more annoyed than scared.

Oh, and did I mention that she was headless? As in having no head atop of her shoulders? Great, huh? Yeah, I was thrilled about this, too, but still annoyed!

So what do I do but do the logical thing and reach towards this lady myself nearly brushing her dress while making the sign of the cross on her belly saying, "In Jesus' Name, get out of here! You are not welcome here!"

I must have done this three or four times before this lady got the picture to leave. So she slowly, and I mean slowly, began to fade away. I was so tired and irritated I didn't even do my usual routine of: "Something freaky just happened here, let me go run to turn a light on!"

Nope, I just rolled over and went back to sleep—yes I was really *that* tired!

I don't know how much more sleep I got in, but it seemed to be rather brief when I felt yet another presence in the room emerge so I rolled over to see what it was this time. Lo' and behold—it 'tis my fair lady once again! Ah, but this time she decides to only float her head in the place that it should have been the last time she showed up!

I remember glancing up at her head floating in mid-air with her round cheeks perfectly visible. I then rolled my eyes in an "oh-brother" kind of way, and put my back to her so I could finally get some sleep! I didn't even bother to give her any more attention.

The next day, even I admit I was a bit surprised at how I reacted to what happened! I kind of wondered what her reasons were for coming my way like that, but then I decided that I really didn't want to deal with any of it anymore. So, I let her and every other spectral visitor out there know that Heidi Hollis was off-limits! I said it out loud, screamed it in my head and echoed it in my soul. I told them all to run and tell their friends, that I was having no more of it—this was *the end*!

I was surprised how well that astral tantrum worked, but it almost worked too well!

I've learned directly because of this incidence, that when one arena gets blocked off in the negative realm that it also makes it harder for the more positive realms to come through, too. So my dreams and visions declined with the uninviting of the ghostly sort, but I honestly didn't mind it since I really needed a break from contemplating otherworldly issues all of the time. I don't think "regular folks" understand how exhausting this sort of thing can be. But I was still sad to see that the angelic and outright positive beings became harder to see then, too.

So then with another leap and bound out of the ghostly afterlife topic, I had come to rest on the topic of aliens. Ah yes, the assortment of strangeness doth continue with me!

How do aliens tie in with all of this stuff involved with my understandings of the paranormal? Well, that is literally another book I wrote called *The Secret War: A True Story About Real Alien War and Shadow People*, but it's slightly part of this one, as well. But all that alien chatter will have to come later on—now is the time for touching on the important parts that shed some light on the main topic at hand and how I arrived here.

Yet and still, how on Earth does one person who was once so outright chicken of paranormal things—happen upon so many peculiar instances? I've asked myself that a lot, too. But then again, odd instances were such a common thing that I didn't really treat it or myself as something out of the ordinary.

Upon working on a television project for Discovery Channel with two wonderful psychics and now good friends of mine, they kept referring to me as a "medium." There was a large group of us working on this show, so I just assumed someone had accidentally told them the wrong thing. So I finally got to mention to them that I was just an experiencer of various paranormal phenomena and was an advocate to bringing paranormal and spiritual awareness to the average person through my writings and lectures.

Then I told these two psychic friends what I'd personally experienced and found answers to concerning all sorts of topics from holy encounters to Shadow People. When I shared on the static between good and bad aliens, they gave each other a look and said, "Well no wonder we thought you were a medium, Heidi, because you are!" They described this is what they did in being able to see a variety of different beings from different realms and were able to harness their abilities to see things when they desired to.

I've said it a million times, but really, who knew I was even stranger than I thought I already was? I never gave myself a title or definition, just that my name was Heidi and I saw whacky things and got answers from beyond normal reach. So, if I'm a medium, well I must be the most thick-headed one out there because I sure don't go straining to see something God doesn't land right in front of my face to see it!

I know there are methods and ways of bringing one's otherworldly senses to be keener and under better control, as my psychic friends explained to me. For all I know, perhaps at some point I'll aim to do such things—but I still don't consider myself to be a psychic or medium. For now I'll just tackle what volts over my fence, one at a time, so I can sic my dogs on it to make sense of it for myself and hopefully others. This life has so many twists and turns, it's a wonder that any of us are ever able to walk erect and straight through any of the doors bestowed in front of us.

Now is my turn to show good balance and gait as I share a bit on one door I crossed into that hid a world of shadow and mystery. This is the door that I wouldn't want anyone to even mistakenly peer through, without having some knowledge and method on dealing with what lies within. But there's always one step that has led to another, which has helped me to better understand what is behind one door after another.

I've had a lot of misfortune in being met with puzzling forces that kept me scratching my head for answers. Yet, with patience and perseverance everything does indeed come into the light of knowledge at some point. So please—allow me to walk you through the darkness I stumbled upon.

Darkness, that has a face and came with *Revelations*.

2

SHADOWY SHADOWS:

The Shadow People

There is always a distorted method to the madness in this paranormal world of all of ours. Seemingly unconnected things somehow find their connection in it and makes keeping an open mind as an essential element to have. Think of it like sending your ex-husband out of the door, only to close the door and turn around and see him with his feet comfortably placed upon your expensive coffee table!

You can turn your back on some of the paranormal things all you would like and cross them off as being nothing but a coincidence or glitch on your way to true balance. Then when you least expect it, you find you need to go back and put up with some of that so-called "nuisance" of unyielding answers that you didn't want to find actually having a connection with the path you are on today!

Definition of the above: Essentially, it gets old and then intriguing again!

So let me gather some more elements from my past of research and odd experiences that has led me to bring forth the yellow brick road of enlightenment on true darkness:

If you've never even heard of me before, the name of a newer phenomenon called "Shadow People" just might ring a bell to the paranormal enthusiasts out there. In 1997, I wrote my first book and *the* very first book about the topic of my experiences in dealing with a presence I personally gave the name to. I didn't know what else to call them but how they appeared to me. So, I figured why get fancy with a name for them and called them as I saw them—Shadow People!

I had actually experienced this shadowy presence for several years prior to writing my first book, *The Secret War.* I originally thought I had one major Shadow People encounter followed by a long hiatus, only for them to resurface again. When actually, they were coming at me in different forms, but were of the same cup of evil. This first encounter is a story you have got to hear if you haven't before:

It happened in 1990 and I've marked it as my first near "crapping of one's pants" incidences. Pardon the sweeping statement, but it was just as moving for me to experience. ☺

I feel I've shared this experience once too many times over the airwaves, but here I go again trotting down memory lane to help paint the picture more clearly:

I was staying at a friend's house, when we decided to go for a walk to her uncle's home. It was broad daylight out, warm and sunny with perhaps a bird whistling nearby—sorry I'm not good for delights while portraying evil. If it helps project the picture better, we were walking along a path that was behind a school that had several trees and bushes lining the way. So anyhow, my friend is walking next to me when I see something from the corner of my vision.

I turned to look as my friend walked on ahead of me and there I saw a huge shadowy thing jump from a bush to a tree and then tree-to-tree, as we walked along our way. I looked on in disbelief and couldn't understand what I was seeing. We soon arrived at our destination and later walked back the way we came, still while the Sun was shining, with birds and the whole bit. As soon as we started walking I saw that shadowy thing again, leaping and bounding along as it followed us back to her house.

By the time we arrived, I was beside myself with mind numbing puzzlement as to what I had just witnessed. Still again, I'm not one to keep things to myself of this magnitude. So, I explained to my friend that I saw something following us, I then got out a piece of paper and drew out this large shadowed figure, which stood around ten feet tall. It was built much like a man, but was big and bulky and had no noticeable neck. I later deemed this one to be called the "Head and Shoulders Shadow"—truly I did. ☺

Here I'm thinking, "I know my friend is going to laugh her head off at me for saying I saw this mythical creature." Instead, she picked up the drawing and hardly gave it a close look. Then she surprised me after she quickly glanced at my scribbled drawing and said nonchalantly, "Oh, that thing. I don't know what that is, but it's been following me since I was a kid."

Can I write "WTF" in this book?!

Either way, that's what I was thinking. I mean, come on, how odd of a statement was that and what an experience! There was still more that happened in dealing with that particular Shadow, but again that's a whole other book—literally (*The Secret War* book I mentioned already)!

Suffice it to say, this was my beginning in seeing these Shadow People. Fortunately—in a sense—things quieted down for a bit until much later when they came at me full force, seemingly on a personal vendetta. How peculiar the story still gets:

While living alone in my own apartment on Milwaukee's college-lively, Eastside, I awoke to hear rustling noises coming from my living room. I sat up in bed and froze for a moment thinking about what to do, because it sounded as if someone had broken into my apartment! With no phone near me at the time, and adrenaline pumping, I soon found myself bolting from my bed to check it out hoping to scare a burglar away or something heroic.

My bedroom door was already wide open, so it's not like I could have hidden from whoever it was. Prior to bolting, I could already see clearly into a portion of my living room, but I saw nothing from my angle. Once I bounded into the living room, there was nothing that could have prepared me for what I was to be met with. What stood before me was something right out of all of the X-files shows with talk of "Little Gray Men!"

There standing before me, were several Gray aliens gallivanting around my apartment moseying through my closet, bookshelf, kitchen and bathroom!

Stunned, but still on my nice little adrenaline rush, I asked these creatures who the heck they were and what the heck they doing going through my stuff?! Oddly enough, the beings sort of stood there in shock themselves! I suppose they were stunned since that whole paralyzing stunt they are known to do to their victims didn't quite work on me. So, essentially I got no response from them but a "dropped-jaw" kind of look.

I then methodically went and grabbed whatever it was I saw these things had in their hands that were mine. For all intents and purposes, it felt like I was scolding little kids for getting into things they had no business getting into. I even had the joy of picking up an odd looking one and shaking it by its little suspenders (or jumpsuit) and asking it what it was doing in my place. For the record, that was the only one wearing any notable clothing and it looked much like the reported half-human and half-alien hybrid beings.

Needless to say, none of them took to liking me very much during my large strides of scolding and taking toys away that weren't theirs to play with. So, soon after introducing the wrath of an angry woman unto them, they all bunched around me and by some means gathered themselves to focus on taking me down.

Somehow, though, this whole scenario wasn't quite a victory for them. Especially being that I'd gotten up and nearly shown them individually the door, even physically rattling one before they scrambled to assemble on what to do. As a strong note, every time something even related to being negative came near me while I was asleep, I bounded awake and was on a holy mission to get rid of them. So no, I'd never been abducted, but yes, they sure did try.

Now then, nearly immediately after I got rid of this round of half-naked aliens scouring my apartment, a new presence took shape. I started seeing these small and sometimes enormous-shadowy masses, invading my small living space. They felt nosey initially, just peering and meandering their way, looking over my shoulder.

I didn't feel anything positive about this presence, and I was struck with the nagging question of what to do about it.

For crying out loud! I'd just gotten rid of some small-Gray creatures—only to have this nuisance show up to take its place?! When I wanted to refer to this presence amongst my friends who were hip to this paranormal stuff, I wanted to have a certain name for them so I didn't always have to explain myself on what I was speaking of.

"Shadow People."

I had no way of knowing, nor a chance of ever even hearing of anyone speak of or call anything even remotely similar to what I had seen or called by that name. Yet, after the publication of my book *The Secret War*, I was stunned to discover that others around the world had already experienced seeing these dark masses, where even some people called them by the same name!

To share more about the nature of these Shadow People—well they are **dark** essentially—end of story.

These things are often reported as being seen from the corner of one's vision, to fully in view, head-on encounters. They are completely black masses, where no light can be seen, but sometimes are partially transparent. They come in all shapes and sizes, from the miniature to the gigantic Shadow. They can even be formed as something disgusting or come in the form of something sweet and furry.

I had personally seen them come in a variety of forms, but one that truly was obscene for me to experience was when they came as giant, hairy spiders! They could be the size of a couple of inches crawling up my arm, to something enormous enough to take up my whole ceiling! Now, as most ladies can stake claim to—spiders are no friend of mine!

If I even walk into a room where I sense a spider glaring at me with their many, beady little eyes—I'm looking for a shoe! God forgive me, but those are one of God's creatures I personally can do without in my own home! To think that there's even something referred to as being a "Clown Spider"—as if a clown *and* a spider aren't scary enough on their own—God had to take it up a notch?! (Okay, so they are really called "Crab Spiders".)

Whatever form these Shadows came in, they were apparently capable of coming and perfecting any shape they wanted to be seen as. They had me fooled into thinking that man-eating, sized spiders truly existed at least for a moment in my home before I realized it was just them being up to their old tricks again. It wasn't like I would round the corner and there was a giant Shadow Spider sitting on my laundry hamper, or anything. When the Shadow Spiders came, they would generally creep around at night while I slept. As I mentioned before, whenever something out of the ordinary was abound, I would bound awake!

These Shadows, of course, didn't stick to only nighttime visits. They would also pop-up during the day, but not nearly as often as during the evening or nighttime. It seemed that they liked to try and blend-in so as not to be spotted while on their little spy trips into my life.

The Shadow People were good at what they did in getting a scare out me, but what were they really doing and why? I didn't find my life to be all that interesting, but I did already have a healthy appetite for exploring and researching paranormal topics. As I briefly mentioned earlier, I especially had a bold interest in the topic of aliens and UFOs, since by that time I'd witnessed seeing some UFOs close up and scolding nine little Grays. Then there was my having dealt with the terrible haunting as a child, the nightmares of my mother, the holy dreams of a Crystal City, and *now* there were these dark things floating and lurking in my home!

When most unlucky, the Shadows would come hulking at me with glowing red eyes, piercing my way; in the form of the Head and Shoulders Shadow. Luckily, when they came in recognizable shapes like that, it was more rare. Usually, when I was still up in the evening I'd see them as small and large Shadow Clouds or Shadow Streaks.

Yet, the question remained in my head, "Why were they here and what were they up to?" Up another road in Paranormal-Ville, I got my answers from yet another odd set of circumstances—via even more aliens!

The Alien Connection

Sit back down, it's okay, I'm not crazy and no one will think you're nuts for reading this book—yet ☺ !

How can I put this plainly? Well, you see I discovered that there truly are two sides to every story. Everyone has heard of the whole alien abduction phenomenon—right? This is where people report being taken and medically experimented on by Gray alien beings who seem to do as they please with these people whether they are for or against what is happening to them.

Yes, there are some people who do not mind their alien experiences and have now changed their minds about their whole view on their abduction encounters. So instead of calling themselves "abductees" they are now saying they are willing volunteers who go along with their once called "alien abductors." Quite a flip-flop from my perspective, being that

I was there in UFO meetings over 15 years ago listening to the horror stories from abductees who wept about their helplessness when heartless aliens approached. Now those tears are dried up where it's all-better now and their sacrifice is their contribution to the survival of humanity?

Okay, okay, I won't get sidetracked here.

Now imagine there being another set of alien beings—positive ones. Aliens who are not so keen to the idea of people being taken against their will in an abducting manner by other races of aliens like the Grays and Reptilians. What if these positive aliens were beings who upheld ethical treatment of soul carrying vessels of all kinds, even humans, who actually spoke of God as their guide for all that they do? One would think if there were such an opposing side of alien beings to the abducting ones, that they may be at odds with each other then. Right? Thus, is the basis of my book *The Secret War* and why it had to be written.

It was actually through this more positive group of alien beings that myself and (unsuspecting and uninterested in the topic) college roommate Samantha and I, got our information on the Shadow People. But it also involved a chunk of intuition, gut feelings, common sense that played into our understandings of these Shadows, as well. Essentially, what we learned is that when I was able to get up and confront that band of Grays who invaded my apartment when I lived alone, they learned that they couldn't fully control me. So, the little losers went back and sent their daddy or personal boss after me—the Shadow People!

Scratching ones head really doesn't help at this point...

I couldn't see any family resemblance going on between the Grays and these large Shadows, nor did I see any similar patterns between them. Grays were physically solid and reportedly took people onboard physical UFOs and performed experiments that usually involved creating human-alien hybrid kids. The Shadows were shadowy, who just lurked, lurked some more, scared me, and gave off a sense of dire evil. They were definitely intimidating, I didn't like them around, and I had some pretty nasty feelings float my way a few times that they wanted to kill me! I later confirmed from the more positive alien contact that these Shadows really did want me out of the picture and dead. It was because I'd seen them, they couldn't control me and I had the potential to tell others about them and beating their tactics. Apparently, they also knew my future before I did about my little book writing habit. ☺ But still, I didn't initially see how they were fully related to aliens.

Naturally, after hearing all of what this positive alien had to say, well it was all too much for me alone to just sit on.

So, soon after gathering the information from my own experiences, alien contacts, blending of friends' experiences and Shadows coming after my life, is when I sat down to write *The Secret War* book. I was still in college and had already decided to take on the hardest degree I could find that didn't involve much math, when I thought to also start my UFO and paranormal discussion group called UFO2U.com. Then came the designing of my first website where I placed some information up about the meetings that my newly founded group would have at the local Eastside library in Milwaukee.

At the time, I was very limited on what information I could share about the Shadows so I didn't initially have anything up on my site about them. It was suggested by the more positive alien beings that nothing be mentioned about what they shared concerning the Shadow People—not until my book was actually published! Apparently, these Shadows didn't want any information put out about them ever and would step up their game against me if I spoke out too soon about them.

After taking only two months to write my book, it took four years before finally finding a way to have *The Secret War* published with all of its intentions! FOUR YEARS! I had to sit on what I knew of these Shadow People for all of that time, nearly bursting my own bubble! Finally, the next step after the book's publication was putting up the drawings of the various forms the Shadows came in.

I just wanted to be sure to provide a visual guide to show what I was talking about to anyone interested in the Shadow People topic. Yes, I know it would have been nice of me to also put those images in the original book. Sadly, I didn't have that option at the time and I knew I could reach more people online with my images—with certainty! As a note, the NEW version of *The Secret War* book (second edition was published in 10/2013 and 5/2014) now does have illustrations.

Backtracking a bit now: During the four-year waiting period to get my book published, the Shadows continued to be crafty and endangering. The haunting game of something dropping from the ceiling onto my bed, shaking it from the weight of what had dropped, was terror striking when I'd awake to see the many eyes and legs of a large Shadow Spider. These and other occurrences helped urge me to want to add an array of additional stories in my book as I waited to publish it. It was a long and drawn out wait and process I had no idea was a part of the publishing world.

Samantha also experienced many of the same peculiar things I did. Sometimes we witnessed things together while hanging out in the living room or kitchen. Other times, we sat in our own individual nightmares as we watched terror come into our rooms at night. Of course, not all of our extraordinary experiences were ones of terror. We also experienced the positive alien beings who educated and warned us on the negative alien beings. Beautiful spheres of light were even seen of various pastel colors, which at times would appear and attack a Shadow! It was as if these various forms of light were outright aiming to get rid of Shadowy entities—right in front of our eyes!

If we didn't witness a paranormal event at the same time, we would be sure to tell the other what we saw or experienced. Sometimes I would wish that I had seen something Samantha experienced, or vice versa. Other times I was super glad to have not been around! There is one particular incidence that led me on the journey to write this very book that you are carefully holding right now, that I am happy to say I had no part in witnessing.

Sadly, I don't know of anyone who could say they wish this incident happened to them with The Hat Man...

3

MAN IN THE ROOM:

Shrieks in the Night

"Ahhhhh!!!" Samantha screamed.

Samantha *always* screamed when she awoke to find something in her room that didn't belong there. I'd actually grown accustomed to her almost nightly shrieks in the middle of the night. In the beginning of her screams cutting through the air, I would bolt upright in my bed and run full speed to her room to see what the heck was going on. Upon reaching her room, by the time I made it, I'd sometimes be bent over nearly holding my knees and panting to catch my breath only to see Samantha already nestling back to sleep! Then she'd just wave me off and tell me she was too tired to talk about whatever had just happened and would say she would tell me about it in the morning.

After what I had just gone through to reach her to save her life?!

I don't see how she thought I could wait to hear what happened to her in the morning. I would, of course, plead and ask her to tell me what was so darn profound that made her screech like that. But, she would hardly ever give-in and just

33

continue to profess that she was too tired to get into the details and would tell me later!

Then when morning came around, I'd anxiously ask about the events that occurred during the night. To my utter dismay, Samantha would be mostly vague and shrug the rest of the story off! She would generally not think much about what she saw and even forgot some of the finer details. Rest assure, that there was always an element of something out-of-the-ordinary lurking about in her room that caused her gut reaction to burst into a scream. Interesting as that was, I thought that all of her encounters must have been absolutely terrifying to her. Then sometimes she would shock me by saying how pleasant some of the things were that she experienced and saw.

"That's just the way I handle seeing whatever is there." Samantha often told me.

I admit that I often got ticked at hearing her nightly death shrieks, startling me to a freakish level of alert! But, everyone has their own way of dealing with these sort of things, it's just not always convenient to others and their own startle reflexes.

On this one particular night in 1995—Samantha's screams did not stop!

I woke up to the initial scream blurted out from Samantha's room. As would be expected—it's the middle of the night and apparently the time to howl at the Moon or something! I swallowed hard and calmed my heart down and took a deep breath. I'd learned to not react physically to pop-up out of my bed by this time, but my racing heart could not be controlled.

"Ahhhhhhhhhhh!!!!" Goes Samantha again. My heart hadn't even settled from the first howl and I think it skipped a beat this time for sure!

"Oh my God! Oh my God! Oh my God!!!" Samantha screamed in terror.

"She's getting unique with this screaming session tonight." I thought to myself.

Before I could even complete that thought, another cry came out that surely sounded more desperate than her usual. "This time someone is REALLY attempting to kill her—because that was a death cry if I ever heard one!" I reasoned to myself.

I jumped up to the side of my bed and paused—she screamed again! I ran out of my bedroom door, through the kitchen and living room and whipped her door open! I was almost certain I was about to enter upon a gruesome scene where an attacker or something was going in for the kill for her to have made the most horrifying screams I'd ever heard in my life!

I'm pretty certain my hand had reached into the room for the light-switch before my body ever made its way in. I flipped the lights on, jumped into the room and gazed madly around the room for the certain predator that was present. To my left—nothing, in front of me—nothing, to my right—fright!

Samantha was perched on her bed, backed into the corner with her arms braced against each wall as if she were trying to shrink into it. Her eyes were wildly searching around the room as she panted and gasped like there was no oxygen available to her. She was no less than hysterical and hardly able to be calmed to even speak clearly at first when I ran into her room.

Then Samantha began repeating in near madness, "The man—the man! He's gone, he's gone—oh my God!"

In Samantha's bedroom she had a door that opened up directly to the porch and she was pointing in the direction of that door as she started trying to explain to me what had happened. The sheer look of panic on her face with floods of tears, told me that someone had actually been in the room. So I immediately tried for the door to make sure it was locked so that the mystery intruder could not return. But the door was already locked! I looked back at Samantha and couldn't figure out how she could have gotten up to lock the door while in her near vegetative state.

I was wholly puzzled!

I needed to find out some answers quickly before I started running out of the door in fear of an assailant wandering in the house! I stood closer to Samantha's bed, trying to soothe her as I started with my barrage of questions. "What man? How'd he get out? Did you lock the door?!" Samantha was shaking and sobbing uncontrollably as I remained standing and shaking trying to figure out what kind of danger we were both still in.

Samantha tried her best to calm herself as she slowly sputtered out, "No—no! He disappeared!"

"He disappeared?" I asked trying to let it sink into my skull.

"Yeah, as soon as you opened the door he just—went away!" Samantha claimed.

"I just came running to what I thought was a murder scene—and it was a supernatural person?" I thought at first.

Samantha put her hand to her chest trying to slow her heart down, "I feel like my chest is going to explode! That was so scary!"

Scary? How could *that* be so scary? After all, Samantha had seen aliens of all sorts—some of the ugliest I'd ever even heard of. She had even seen various ghosts, a winged creature that hurled rocks and heard the growl of an unseen Hell Hound. Then here she sees a man and she's terrified like this? None of this made any sense to me at all.

"What was so horrible about this man?" I asked.

"He wouldn't go away!" She demanded. "When I scream and it's something bad, they usually just go away!"

Great! Now I knew why she really did these movie-blood-curdling-death screams! This was her defense against them? So my attempts of sleeping through the night weren't even a consideration—a typical roommate scenario we would have to discuss later.

"Not this *man*, though! He woke me up somehow and when I saw him I screamed, and he didn't even move—he just stood there staring at me!"

I was still not getting the full impact of what she was saying. She and I have been through and seen SO much; I couldn't understand what the big deal was. "Okay and then what happened?" I figure there *had to* be more somehow.

"That's all he did! He was *so* freaking-evil feeling!"

Samantha then started to try and drive the reality of this man into my mind, "He was really tall, slender and he wore a three-piece suit with a white shirt under it. He even had a pocket-watch looped and hanging on his hip, it was gold from what I could see. He even had on a long trench coat on and he was wearing this flat hat on his head!"

"A hat?!" I thought that was kind of funny.

"Yeah, it was like the hat that Zorro wears—you know the guy from the movies and TV show!"

Now I thought that part was really funny, because she was actually describing a Zorro looking character already.

"He was all dressed in black, too! He was really pale white and had a goatee of a beard. The worst part of it is—he had solid-black eyes!"

Chills hit me. She had my attention even more fully, now!

"Oh my God!" I exclaimed. "That's nasty!"

Almost as if Samantha knew that the full impact of what she had just experienced, hadn't quite hit me yet, she leaned in closer. "He was SO real and SO evil, Heidi! I didn't think he was going to leave—until you came in."

Puzzling.

Samantha went to sleep on the living room futon for the rest of the night, though she hardly slept. I didn't get the best sleep myself. I did my best to tell myself that it was just another one of those odd things that tends to stop by my apartment from time-to-time. I had already been dealing with aliens, ghosts and Shadow People for quite some time already. So this was no big deal to have a sharply dressed phantom stop by, forgetting his manners to remove his hat in a gentlemanly fashion as is expected when indoors.

The next morning, Samantha continued to tell me more details—a rarity for her:

"There was some light coming in from the streetlights, so I could see this guy pretty clearly. He was standing in the shadows halfway, but I could see him really good still. He was so real, so solid and so evil!"

I had never seen such a thing before, personally, but I did believe Samantha fully about her account. I just didn't have any reference point to refer to for this man in the hat. Samantha then did a quick sketch of the man on her sketchpad, in pencil. She happens to be a more than exceptional artist, where in a matter of minutes, I was able to get a good idea of what this man looked like.

He looked ordinary for the most part, but he had a pointed chin and nose. Samantha shaded a lot of him in with the shadows of the room that overcast him a bit. We both talked on him quite a bit that day in-between going to our separate colleges and jobs.

"What a bold Shadow Person he was," was the consensus between us.

I could never figure out why a variety of dark things seemed to come at Samantha so much harder sometimes. However, she did have a unique gift in seeing through the veil of this life better than most. Her ability to spot out things was so heightened, I honestly just figured she had come across something so perfectly rare that it couldn't and wouldn't be repeated elsewhere.

At least I had hoped.

The alien beings Samantha and I were in contact with didn't volunteer any information on this man with the hat. I don't recall us bringing up the topic with them either, being that we were often being bombarded with odd entities and confrontations, our minds were already full enough. If I am ever in touch with Samantha again, I will be sure to ask her more about her perspective on him.

Ah yes, for those of you who are reading this and have also read *The Secret War* book, here's some info you might appreciate. I'm sure some of you have wondered what has happened to our relationship with the chatty alien being since the publishing of that book. The revealing answer is: Not much. To be more specific, the positive being we had the most contact with went by the name of "Cafth" and he has moved on due to some unfortunate circumstances. The communication we had with him went something like this: Samantha essentially had direct contact with him and then she relayed the messages he wanted to pass along, though I had personally seen him, as well.

What took place involving Samantha and Cafth's departure is a very long and interesting story, with a touch of sadness. A story that I will be sure to share when it's appropriate. It's one of those stories that I'd like to give time to hopefully remedy itself for more positive things. For now, this man in the hat takes precedence.

There was no knowing that Samantha's encounter with this stranger in her room would lead me into another unexplored area of the paranormal realm—yet again! This man in the hat wasn't a casual encounter, nor happen stance. I'm now certain he had a front row seat in watching us scramble and get things wrong and fall apart. Lots of adjustments were needing to be made and prayers needing to be said.

What I thought was random—wasn't! What I thought had no pointed answer—did! What I thought just couldn't be—was!

4

SHADOW PORTRAITS:

Mug Shots

Flash-forward four years later after Samantha's man in the hat encounter and I was finally able to speak freely! That's because *The Secret War* book was out and so was the secret about Shadow People existing in our world. It was time to let everything be known about them, so hitting conferences and conventions to speak publicly for the first time was a huge goal. I also aimed to be on every radio show that would have me and I was super excited about the process—it was all so new to me!

UFO conferences were what I was aiming to speak at, but they still weren't fully biting on what I was presenting. Besides the topic I was highlighting, I was young, a woman, slightly tanned, and I often had a "good time" chatting about anything peculiar. This all spelled that I wasn't quite part of the "typical club members" where such things were presented mostly by men over the age of 50 who kept a straight face with monotone lectures.

That just had to be said (or written), just to keep it real. Though it does seem that slowly the tides of change are washing ashore—finally!

Yet, I did have the awesome privilege of going on some of the top radio programs out there where I was heard across the globe and got to present a topic no one had ever heard of before. But I don't recall getting any invites unless I did the calling and asking to be squeezed into a lecture program, at my own expense, to get to the place in hopes of being heard and helping others. When I did actually get to speak instead of sitting in the vendors rooms at my self-paid table, with a stack of my books in-tote, audience members often said they were relieved and excited to hear about something new and informative.

Yet and still, organizers of UFO conferences weren't interested in much of what I had to share. In fact, I overheard one organizer say to another, "Shadow People? That's straight out of science fiction like on *Babylon 5!*" For those of you who don't know, that's an old television series and even I didn't know there was an alien race on there called "Shadows."

I was stunned.

Especially being that I was at a UFO conference when I overheard this and tons of people in the world think of UFOs as being all hoaxed! Oddly, I somehow expected narrow-mindedness to be less prevalent in an already shunned field. It was fully surprising to me and it made me realize why less progress has been made in the world of the unknown. How can any progress be made when there's inner-fighting going on?

Speaking of science fiction: Science Fiction Conventions were a whole other-awesome story! ☺

They were highly receptive and open to hearing about the possibilities of real alien beings visiting our planet—even if I called some "Shadow People." I always got to lecture at the Sci-Fi conventions where I received a free vendor table and was warmly greeted by the organizers who didn't judge me based on who or what I was. Besides all of that, I got to hang out and meet some of my favorite science fiction stars who made my trip worth it—though I did still usually pay my way there (though not always—here's a warm hello to my friends at Mis-Con).

It was my lecturing at the science fiction conventions that really helped me build character. It also let me know that there was acceptance out there among the worldly population and not just those who directly sought out the topics I covered. Going to UFO conferences taught me a lot, too, of course. I loved meeting some of the awesome people I did. Having a meeting of the minds, depth of thought and contemplation towards our topics of interest, all helped to inspire me in irreplaceable manners. It was my meeting of these people at UFO conferences and sharing of stories that also helped me realize that UFO conferences were not necessarily presenting topics of interest to the audience. Often times, the same rehashed topics were presented by the same man, showing the same images and sharing the same information we have known about for years.

Soon, meeting the people who attended these conferences took precedence at any event I went to. Talking, sharing and learning from each other is all that was needed and it was where the real growth came from. I was always eager to listen to others and hoped that I was helping in some way by my own sharing. My sharing also included making better use of my websites by putting more and more information on them—as I created more sites to accommodate various other topics that I covered.

I was SO nervous and anxious to begin telling my story, since I was SO limited on speaking of Shadow People for SO long. When I finally did start talking on Shadow People, my main UFO and paranormal group discussion site was up for four years already, www.UFO2U.com. It was nerve racking to be out of the gates after thinking over it all for years on how to present this stuff and hoping I would do it right!

Samantha, being a graphic artist on top of everything else she can sketch, paint or sculpt; took on creating images of the various forms that we had seen Shadow People take on. These were the forms that either she or I had seen these Shadows take on, though we were told via Cafth that these beings could take on most any form. For a site fully dedicated to Shadow People, Samantha created simplistically accurate graphics that we posted up online and I used in my PowerPoint presentations: Head and Shoulders Shadow, Cat Shadow, Spider Shadow, Black Cloud Shadow, Shadow Streak, Shadow Spheres, Hooded Shadows and Hat Man Shadow.

Just to be clear, at this point I still hadn't known of anyone having experienced these Shadow People outside of myself and Samantha (and the friend who had one follow her years earlier). So up went the graphics, then I started doing the radio show and lecture circuits. Then after doing the fantastically popular Coast to Coast AM radio show with George Noory— this is when I learned many others were experiencing these same beings in a similar fashion as myself! Whether I was talking to people directly or receiving emails of people's stories, each one I heard of truly hurt me to learn of.

To me it was like sharing that you had a horrible and ongoing nightmare, then when you finally turn to tell someone about it they stop you mid-sentence to finish telling your story for you! But how could that be? I knew that at some point these dark creatures would rear their ugly heads, as per our conversations with Cafth that this nightmare would spread. We had never thought to ask if the nightmare had already begun, though!

It was horrifying to learn of and the first of these revelations began close to home:

My sister Keisha had unexpectedly stopped by my house and I was more than glad because she hadn't seen or even known about my book being published. Because of the book's content, I knew my family wouldn't fully understand why I had written it. Besides, I didn't want to tease them with my not being able to disclose the full contents of the book prior to its publication. The same went for the new Shadow People website, and as luck would have it, my sister showed up the day that I put up the new graphics of the Shadows. So, when Keisha came to the door I was eager to show her the new addition to my website.

"Hey sis! Oh—you've gotta see the new graphics on my website I just got up!" I told her excitedly as I gave her a big hug and pulled her inside.

Keisha is the youngest in my large and blended family of 12 siblings. I'm the second youngest; we are close in age and were often dressed to look like twins growing up. This clothing choice was not always something we liked to do, but we were best friends growing up and still are. The odd thing is, she and I have a connection that we really cannot explain.

She used to finish my sentences growing up and now we just do things that are frightening similar: One time, I was just about to order some new furniture for my living room. A couple of weeks later I walked into her home to find that same set of furniture she had just purchased in her living room. Another time, I loved a certain cartoon character in a movie so much, that I bought the action figure of it and set it to the left of my television in my living room. Upon going to Keisha's place, I saw that she had bought the *same* figure and placed it to the *right* of her television in her living room. Then once, I had a dream of being pregnant—but it was her who was actually pregnant! She has also seen UFOs, ghosts, spirits and some other unexplained events involving some psychic phenomenon.

To be blunt, she's nearly as weird as I am, but I think I've got a few steps up on her!

After I pulled Keisha inside of my house, I had her follow me into my office as she started to tell me, "Hey, I had something weird happen to me. I don't know..."

I quickly sat down at my computer and started to busily pull up my website as I continued to listen to her. Keisha started, "About a week ago, something was in my basement. I had just gone down to get my laundry..."

I finally got to my site and clicked open the gallery of Shadow People drawings. I was so proud and full of smiles as I did the big reveal to my little sis.

"That's it!" She exclaimed.

"That's what?" I was miffed.

"That's what I saw! What is that thing?!" Keisha was pointing excitedly straight at The Hat Man Shadow drawing. I simply froze.

"You saw this guy—but how?"

"That's what I was telling you just now! A week ago I had to go into the basement to get my laundry. So I walked downstairs and was just about to step off from the last step as I was looking towards the dryer. That's when I got this eerie feeling and looked up and saw this extremely tall and dark shadow of a man literally just rise up from behind the dryer! The fear—I mean—I just dropped everything and ran as fast as I could up the stairs and scared your niece so bad that she started running with me to the other end of the house!"

"What—? He just rose up out of nowhere? Is there space behind the dryer for a man to stand?" I asked.

"No! The dryer is right up against the wall. It looked like a shadow was cast of a man—who was wearing a hat—of all things! This rimmed hat! It looked like he had a cape, maybe, too! It was such a solid shadow—extremely dark!"

I was dumbfounded, especially when she had more to say:

"Then a couple of days ago, I was driving in my car and it was still light outside, but raining a little. I was looking in my rearview mirror; when I thought I saw something dark go past my view. It was weird and I got this eerie feeling again. So, I looked over my right shoulder towards the back and there he was just sitting there! I screamed and had to turn back forward to see the road and looked back again and he was gone!

"He just rose up like he did before in the back seat, right before my eyes, like he did before! Then, he just disappeared! That time I could really feel him—he just made you so fearful and unsafe! He was so evil! As soon as I could, I pulled over, hopped out and just had to take a minute to get the fear out of me."

My stunned state turned into asking for more details. "Could you see what he was wearing or anything?"

Keisha began, "He was wearing that same, old-fashioned type of rimmed hat that no one wears anymore. This time he was really solid, too, but you could slightly see through him. It seemed like he had something draped over his shoulders—and he had RED EYES! He just freaked me out so bad—scared me really, really bad!"

"My poor sis!" I thought. But I really didn't know how to filter what she was telling me.

Today, she informed me how she never went back into that basement alone again and how she still gets an ominous feeling whenever she talks about it. Needless to say, she never really spoke much about it again until I asked her to for this book.

I couldn't understand why this thing had come to my sister this way, but I oddly felt responsible. I had never even spoken of Shadow People to my family or really anyone, yet. I hadn't realized it on that day, or for many days to come that this was to be the first stitch in a string of patches and patterns that would emerge concerning this Shadow Man. I hadn't gotten to the point of even getting angry about this whole phenomenon, yet. It was disturbing, of course, and not something I wanted others to have to deal with.

Since myself and Samantha were still in contact with Cafth at the time, he informed us that darkness would attack anyone close to us. He expressed how this would especially happen more as we became more knowledgeable and became less accessible to the darkness. So, we were told to be sure to inform people we knew to try and keep strong in the face of these horrible things coming their way. It was a daunting task, because I was still so very new to even talking to others about the Shadow People. So, I don't think I did very well in enlightening people to their threatening presence and so the darkness continued to encroach upon others I knew.

What a terrible circumstance to be in and from the sounds of it, apparently my initial guilty reaction to what my sister told me was accurate.

Crap!

5

THE HAT MAN:

Calling It As I See It

Initially, I only had Samantha's one encounter with The Hat Man Shadow to go on in putting his drawing up on my site. Then nearly as quickly as I put up his drawing I got immediate feedback about it—with the first being from my sister, unfortunately. Totally not what I would have ever expected! This is the original graphic placed upon my website, though it did at one point show the facial features of him having a goatee, pointed chin, wearing a three-piece suit, a tie and brandishing a chained watch. Somehow, overtime, all of the copies that I have of the graphic no longer shows the details it once did.

After hearing my sister's story, from that moment on I started receiving reports of similar encounters. I was less shocked by them after Keisha's story, but I was shocked, nonetheless. I then started reaching out to people via an online column, talking on radio shows and the lecture circuit in hopes of shedding light on the topic. It didn't take long before I was completely bombarded by people telling me their personal stories and attacks by Shadow People.

I listened and I learned.

I presented Shadow People as the connection between the various types of aliens victimizing people here on Earth via abductions and other intruding tactics. Shadow People were these negative aliens' puppeteers, taking over their very willpower to do their biding. I had ghost hunters telling me or telling others in a ridiculing fashion, that Shadow People were merely the shadow of a ghost—literally!

I listened, but I had already a fair understanding about these Shadow People from personal experience, common sense and a connection to an outer (alien) source. It didn't hurt me to hear what others and researchers had to say, but it hurt me

50

to even imagine how unprepared these people may be when faced with one of these beings.

Then the ghost hunters started to get their introductions to Shadow People—face-to-face. I was frightened to hear of their fright!

More and more I started getting stories of these ghost hunters telling me how they assumed Shadow People to be just ghosts or associated to them somehow—UNTIL they met one! It was only then that they knew there was no mistaking that this was a whole other twist in the paranormal world! It was horrifying to see the trend start to change out there in the midst of so many ghost hunters out in the field. These dark menaces were taking up residence in the usual haunts and now, suddenly, making themselves more known.

The Hat Man Shadow reports continued to come in, but they were more scattered at first. The emails and comments I received came in great numbers due to the gallery of Shadow People graphics on my website. I got more reports about the Head and Shoulders Shadow than anything and that was disturbing enough.

It was a strange path for me to take to have to address Shadow People all of the time all of a sudden. My initial, big interest had always been on the alien phenomena going on out there. I found the alien-human interactions to be so interesting. I wanted to learn about all that was being said and whether they were good or bad aliens doing the communicating with people. I was always eager to keep my ears and mind open, because at times, some positive morsels of information were being shared by various beings. But when I began dishing on Shadow People, the alien comments and stories sent to me started to gradually dwindle down.

I created a site called Alien Advice (www.AlienAdvice.com), where I was addressing the many emails that came in to me about a whole variety of topics. I would get so many stories sent to me where the people were just asking for advice on what to do in the face of their alien encounters and Shadow People encounters, that this website became essential. I at first was addressing so many similar questions and scenarios that I know I was repeating myself on a regular basis. So, as the emails started coming in I asked permission to post them online and answer them there instead via email (as I had been doing). I wasn't a guru of any sort, but in compiling what I had learned over the years and via Cafth, I did my best to help if I could.

Eventually, Shadow People were all that people were emailing me about. Their stories were fascinating and all—but there was never anything positive about them coming to people and they didn't speak most of the time. As the Shadow People stories dominated my inbox, Hat Man Shadow stories were bunched in the mix, as well. Just as I got comfortable with the realization that I would be dealing with the Shadow People as a whole from now on, something changed.

I would read the emails, then draw from my Shadow People knowledge and relay whatever I could to whomever was asking me questions in the emails sent:

"Dear Heidi, The Shadow jumped on my chest and started to choke me—what do I do?"

"Well, Mr. So-and-so, you do A. to equal B. and then we are at C." I'd respond.

Then, I got to the emails that left me with my hands not able to touch the keyboard due to being dumbfounded.

Much like:

Dear Heidi,

I was maybe 5 years old when The Hat Man started to visit me. Every night I would lay in the top bed of my bunk bed and watch as my door would crack open for him to creep inside. As high up as I was, I would still have to look up to see him and I would freeze in horror at the sight of him!

He moved faster than anything humanly could, as he'd spring towards me. He would then say, "One day I will have you!" Then he would put his hands around my neck and begin to choke me! I would shoot straight up in bed screaming at the top of my lungs—then he'd just disappear!!!

My mom would just dismiss it all, though she had taken me to doctors to try and help with my nightly outbursts. She eventually grew tired of it and took the light bulb out of the lamp in my bedroom so I couldn't get up to turn it on all night long. One night, she even locked the door on me with The Hat man inside of the room with me!

I heard The Hat Man come close to me and say, "Now I've got you!"

It was on this night that my mother didn't hear me scream. So she came into the room to check on me only to find my body was pushed through the narrow, wooden rails of my bunk bed—hanging by my neck!

It took my mom and three of her male friends to pry the wood apart to get me out from between the wooden planks! Afterwards, they found large hand marks around my neck in bruises. They did CPR on me to bring me back to life and I woke up screaming, "He almost had me!"

I slept with my mom every night after that until we moved out of that place. I never saw him again!

Um. This wasn't sounding very typical of what I called the "Shadow People."

Then I'd get the email that says, "Heidi, that man on your site in the hat—I've known him for years!"

"Uh, what?!" I didn't know how to respond to those sorts of claims initially. So, I sat on it for a long while.

Getting an email is one thing, but then things got personal, yet again:

Fresh out of college, I was moved and living in a new apartment with a good friend I will call "Golda." I was still not practicing as an occupational therapist because of a few different things going on, one being that I was focused on writing and getting word out on Shadow People. By this time everyone who knew me, knew of my supernatural ties and writings. So, Golda knew me well enough to be prepared for some odd things to potentially come her way in sharing a place with me.

Golda had not experienced anything out of the ordinary before this, so the experience I'm about to relay here was more than a shock for her:

I was in the kitchen, washing dishes, which is probably my least favorite thing on the planet to do! So I wasn't thrilled, but it was just one of those things we all do.

I had just picked up a plate, when I got the strangest sensation come over me that caused me to suddenly say something loud and oddly stated: "Golda! What are you thinking?!"

She didn't respond. Then again I heard myself belt out loudly as if someone else said it, "Golda! What are you thinking?!"

There was such an urgency in me to get her to immediately redirect herself, her thoughts, her mind and soul to not rationalize whatever was taking place. I dropped everything, barely shaking my hands of the suds bound up to my elbows. I quickly bolted down the overly long hallway that led to her bedroom and sprang her halfway, opened door fully open! I said it again, "Golda! What are you thinking?!"

It seemed so forced and unlike my own words coming out of me, but it felt like the soul of me was on high alert to rectify whatever was amiss.

Golda was sitting on her bed studying for class and quickly looked up at me and oddly said, "I think one of your friends wants to talk with you."

"What friend? Who are you talking about?!" I was nearly demanding.

"I don't know. I was sitting here studying when I suddenly saw this man in my mind. I'm wide-awake sitting here and he just shows up and is waving for me to come on and follow him. I stopped looking at my book and could distinctly still see him with my eyes open! I watched him walk away from me and turn into this dark alley and when I got close to it, I looked down it and saw him still waving me to come on and follow him.

"I thought about it and then realized that he must be wanting you to follow him, because this weird stuff is all for you! So, I thought to get you or go down the alley myself—but then I heard you scream out to me.

"The guy came closer to me to keep waving me towards him—insisting like. I told him I would go get you so you could talk to him. He kept getting closer and you yelled again. He was just about to reach me when you came in here! He then seemed to just go away—just leave my view and mind!"

"That was no "friend" of mine waving you to come down a dark alley! What did he look like?" I insisted.

"He was dressed old-fashioned, with a black suit, trench coat and with this hat on his head."

My mind collapsed in on itself.

Apparently, that creep had crept in for another look-see at those who are close to me!

I had learned by that time to inform people to take heed of anything odd coming their way and Golda was more than informed. However, she never took my topics very seriously. I asked her what would make her even give this glimpse in her mind a second look. She said it was so profound to even see something like this that it caught her curiosity. She was one to never hold back any punches in letting me know that these sorts of odd experiences were reserved for "freaks" like me!

What can I say about statements like this, but that you've just got to love your friends!

I was used to this sort of banter though, it was actually pretty typical until my friends partook and drank from the same cup of "weirdness" themselves! I always loved being in the front row to watch how it changed their perspective of the world, but I always hoped that they would experience something paranormally positive than the negative. However, as luck would have it, the positive stuff would usually come after a negative event.

Golda told me that this guys' plight was so strong and dire, that had she not heard me yell for her she was sure she would have gone towards him. Then it finally dawned on her, "Hey—what made you call-out for me like that anyways? Why did you ask, 'What are you thinking?' How'd you know I was thinking anything?"

"I don't know—it was weird—I knew I just had to call out to you and get to you as soon as possible!"

"Just another freak trick!" Is what I should have told her! ☺ I didn't want to freak her out too badly, though.

She was pretty shaken up in being convinced now and having no doubts how other powers could get into her head—literally! I felt bad, then vindicated all at the same time. Yet, I didn't know what this had all meant at the time and this is surely nothing I would have wanted to wish upon her or anyone to experience. I wondered what might have happened had she gone down that alley. Then the scary thought came to mind of how many people actually did follow him and were never able to tell anyone. Was it a point of no return? I was glad to not know, but for other's sake, I wish I had a better understanding.

Skip ahead a few months, and Golda and I were heading to hang out with some friends. It was daylight out still as we jumped into her car. I had borrowed her car earlier, so she had to make some adjustments to her seat. She made some smart-alecky remark about how I liked to drive laid back so far that it was a miracle I could see over the steering wheel. We were the same height, 5 feet 8 inches, so I couldn't understand how or why she'd cram her knees up to her chin to drive!

We had a good laugh about it as she scooted her chair up with a loud click. Being thorough in her adjustments she then reached for her rearview mirror—when she screamed at the top of her lungs! My heart thudded and then seemed to kick me for having these friends who liked to scream at inopportune moments!

"The-the man!" Golda stuttered. "From your site! He's in the back seat!" She hollered!

By the time she sputtered out those words and I turned about and she turned around—he had vanished!

"He was solid-and-and—real!" Golda wasn't one to frighten easily and she always liked to apply logic to all scenarios.

"Wow—two unexpected encounters—how do you explain this one?" I asked her in a funny-rotten tone that only a friend can get away with. I was especially curious what she thought about odd phenomena in general now that she had her feet wet in it twice. But by this time, she was beginning to question what she had originally experienced, though I knew she accepted the reality of what took place. But I also knew that she needed to tell herself something else must have occurred to keep her mind at ease.

Golda didn't have any way of denying what she saw and she never recanted it. Proudly, she didn't fear for herself in the face of what she saw, either. Though it shook her to the core of her, as she expressed how absolutely evil this guy's presence was. Luckily, her experiences didn't end there as she was introduced to some of the most incredible stories I have ever heard. One of her encounters involved Jesus! The other encounter was a very involved "waking dream" with Moses that left a footprint on our window ledge (that was four feet off the floor) in the living room!

Yes, I know—quite different stuff there. Think about it though: If the evidence of negative things are accepted and seen, trust me, there is a polar opposite that is much more powerful and present. This is why I called my second book, *Jesus Is No Joke: A True Story of an Unlikely Witness Who Saw Jesus*—because He isn't a joke! ☺

So, back to where I was:

This Hat Man Shadow had come close enough where I should have been able to smell his breath from the backseat! Luckily for me though—I had not seen him. But why? What was he up to and why was he doing things that just seemed so "in your face" or behind my back, at least?

Without planning to, I started dropping the name "Shadow" from his name and just started calling him "The Hat Man." It just seemed pointless anymore, but for my sites and presentations, I left the name Shadow on there at the end. But, I knew more and more that putting "Shadow" on there was becoming less and less appropriate....

Another case and point story:

Dear Heidi,

When I was around five years old, I woke up to a man in my bedroom. He wore a black fedora hat and black overcoat. His skin was pale and grayish. I could see his face pretty clearly.

When I more fully woke up—he left my room. I was extremely scared so I ran into my parent's bedroom to wake them both up. The closet door inside of their bedroom was wide-open. When I passed by the closet I sort of glanced inside of it —the man was standing in the closet!

He stood almost to the top of the closet doorframe, so he had to be between 6.5 to 7 feet tall! His face was old and reminded me of the older Boris Karloff in looks (he played the original Frankenstein in the old movies). He had huge-hound dog eyes and had a faint, gray and white mustache against his pale-grayish skin.

As I walked past the closet and saw him now standing in there—I freaked out and quickly tried waking my parents up. I shook my dad to get up, because of the man in their closet. My dad awoke along with my mom and they turned on the light to find that there was no man in the closet. I tried to explain that he must have left as I was trying to wake them up.

I always believed I wasn't having a nightmare, even though my parents tried to convince me otherwise.

My entire life I kind of thought that he might have been a predator or kidnapper, since I always did think of the event as a real occurrence. I even told my wife about it, as it was a childhood memory that had always stalked me. Then while surfing around the web I stumbled upon your site and here others have had similar encounters.

I didn't feel as if he was menacing other than him being a strange man in the house. But it did scare me as a child, enough for me to remember it quite vividly 45 years later...

Memories of a nightmarish man that lasts for years—with just a glimpse of him? That should send shudders among the masses to even catch a whisper of. I know it did for me and the shudders never seem to end anymore.

6

CONTEMPLATIONS:

What The Heck?!

I moved out of the country!

Not to outrun this newly renamed "Hat Man" thing, of course, but to go to live my dream and hang out in Australia! I moved to Victoria in Melbourne on Flemington Road, to be exact. Most people I meet in the United States all say that the "Land Down Under" is their number one place they would like to visit or live—I was no different.

Just prior to my big move, I finally began to practice as an occupational therapist, which was delayed five years after I graduated. At the time, I was already fairly focused on speaking out on Shadow People and putting word of my first book out there. So, there I was finally working via a therapy contracting company on an assignment that was to last only four months at a rehabilitation center and then off to Oz I would go.

My contract was nearing its completion at this center, when the topic came up of "spooky stuff." One of the other therapists I was working with started talking about a scary movie they had just seen. So I shared how I didn't mind a good scary movie—when I had in fact seen most, if not all movies of that genre out there.

When you are a lady and you even share a little bit of information about loving horror movies, it can raise a few eyebrows. Then for me, this sort of chat usually leads into sharing my whole horrifying background. Up to this point, the other therapists didn't know about my extra-curricular activities. I wasn't hiding it; it just never came up where a need to share this info was needed or necessary. Like I've mentioned, I know how to clear a room when I want to—but I usually reserve that for family and friends and most times unintentionally (though I do tend to sneak in some room-clearing stories). ☺

So, I didn't interject much into the conversation, as it was, until something unexpected happened. One of the therapists chimed in to say that they lived a horror movie for themselves and no longer cared to see spooky movies. So, you know I had to ask why and how:

"I lived in a sorority house while in college and I had been living in a smaller room when one of the sorority sisters graduated and gave up her larger room to me. I was glad to get it, but there was a strange feel about her room. It even seemed to always be colder in that room, for some reason, too.

"My first night sleeping in there I didn't get to finish unpacking, I was too tired to do it all. I went to sleep and woke up because I could feel something was in the room with me. When I turned to look—right there standing next to my bed was this ghost!"

The rest of the therapists and I shared her fright at how horrible that must have been for her. We joked how he must have been an ex-boyfriend buried in the walls of the sorority house, discarded and was now a nasty little secret of the house! The therapist sharing the story was serious and quick to point out that it was a mystery, fully. Especially, because no guys had ever lived at the place since it had always been a sorority house.

"Well what did he look like?" Another therapist asked.

"That was even stranger, he was wearing like this old-fashioned suit, with a long, black trench coat, or cape!" My heart dropped into the stinky part of my tennis shoes, as if there's any difference in any part of them.

"Was he wearing a hat?" I asked, nearly not wanting to as I kicked the frog out of my throat in order to expose myself for who I was.

"Yeah! What the—how the—who the—?" She asked something like that anyways.

The G-Rated version: "Wait—how'd you know that? Yeah, he was wearing this rimmed hat on his head, a fedora or something like it."

I told her how a few people I personally knew had seen the same thing and that I had a drawing of him online she could check out. The disturbing look across her face grew more intense as she shared more, "That wasn't the last time I saw him—he came almost every night! He would just stare at me and I always knew when he was there. I told the other sorority sisters about it and they didn't believe me. I finally moved into another room when another girl said she'd trade with me. That same night he showed up to her! Finally someone else was convinced he existed!

"That girl saw him again the next night and then she moved in with another girl in the house into a larger room. No one wanted that room after that and it remained empty the rest of my time living there. I always wondered who he was. He was so evil feeling and those black eyes were so hard to forget!"

My heart sank to a new low; this wasn't an email, or a close friend, or family member this time telling me their story. I was looking into the eyes of a person who told me a story of their personal horror and bewilderment of how reality can be changed in an instant of unfamiliarity. This was outside of myself and words written up on a screen, or hearing from family and friends whom I was familiar with their expressions of fear.

I saw it, I saw it, I saw it.

I saw a glimmer of what was going on with The Hat Man and tucked it away in my mind.

I was soon off to Australia—with no job, no intentions and as they say there, "No worries, mate!"

I just wanted to explore the possibilities of living in a new country as a permanent resident and take it all in. I had a lot of time on my hands, so I took to writing right away while I travelled around and hung out with new friends. I had always gotten a lot of emails, but regrettably, I wasn't always able to respond and even read all of the emails I had received. However, while in Melbourne, emails were all I seemed to read while getting some new writings done.

Sinister, telltale signs of this Hat Man dangled in front of my eyes, as I read more emails based on encounters with him. I looked at what was transforming into another phenomenon outside of Shadow People, but I simply didn't want to admit to it. It wasn't admission to being wrong that I was afraid of. I didn't want to admit to myself, or anyone else that something even worse than the Shadow People existed and even co-existed in their presence:

Dear Heidi,

My wife and I have had experiences with several types of Shadow People. We have even tried to contact several demonologists for their help, but we have had no luck going this route in getting rid of this presence.

For three years, my wife and I have been experiencing poltergeist activity directly from Shadow People. We feel like we are losing our minds.

I don't know how else to say this, but that I have even been bitten by a black shadowy cloud. My wife was once woken up by a 9-foot tall Shadow Person, that had either horns or a hat. My wife woke me up while yelling, "In the name of Jesus Christ I rebuke you!"

It immediately left.

I have been personally thrown onto my bed by one of the "Head and Shoulders Shadows." But get this: The Shadow Person SPOKE!

As he was throwing me onto my bed, which woke up my wife, it screamed, "Jesus Christ has no power over me!"

It was stories like this, with a combination of entities coming forward with so much defiance against Jesus that got me to sink back in thought and contemplations.

As the emails mounted up in my mind, I thought quietly to myself about what was going on and why this Hat Man had been encountered so widely. I knew that I needed to stop looking away from what I was seeing and at least address it in some form. Initially, I kept it all quietly to myself. Especially since I was never surrounded with people who could relate to me or my topics, anyways. The closest people to me were the folks involved in my paranormal and UFO discussion group (UFO2U), who all lived quite a distance away.

Yet and still, I hardly spoke of new things I was pondering. Doing that was a hard lesson learned to avoid weird judgment being placed on me, or even having outright words of mine being borrowed by others and published—literally! Spreading knowledge is the ultimate goal, of course, but it was an odd predicament to be in.

So, I slowed down in sharing as much as I used to. But I was feeling so heavy in seeing the pattern that I was seeing in these Hat Man encounters, that I knew I couldn't sit idly by for long. I always say: "With knowledge comes responsibility."

Finally, I took in The Hat Man emails and got the itching to find more answers via someone else who could actually relate to what I was observing. So I emailed someone—Lorraine Warren! Yes, I went to the queen of the paranormal herself! Lorraine is one of the few people in the world whom I felt could give me some insight like no other. Her and her late husband had crossed into some of the darkest corners of our globe when it came to negative entities. I think all I need to say are the names "Amityville Horror" or "The Conjuring" and it might ring a bell about who she is.

So, I sent a sincere email to her website saying who I was and how I had come across a phenomenon that was brand new. I then stated how I was needing some help in perhaps defining this phenomenon and wondered if she had heard of it before. I was pleasantly surprised to get a response from her equally impressive nephew, John Zaffis. He suggested that I contact her directly via her phone and gave me her number!

Say what?! I was simply ecstatic!

I had a "flat-mate" (i.e. roommate) while living in Melbourne, you might know by now named Golda! She was there gaining her Master's degree, which made it a ton easier for me to move there since I knew someone. Golda asked if I'd like to come and she didn't have to ask again! I didn't want to freak her out about The Hat Man she had already been met with, so I didn't say anything in regard to my contemplations and efforts for answers on him.

After I got settled for a couple of months in our shared space, I noticed Golda had been looking tired for a couple of days. The day I received the email from John Zaffis, Golda went to bed early. I had already started writing on my new book projects; *Picture Prayers* (now entitled *How To Pray Like The Angels*) and *Jesus Is No Joke.* About an hour after Golda went to bed, she came knocking on my door and sat down on the floor, folding her legs and leaned against the wall.

"Hey—what's up? I thought you were going to bed early." I knew that I wasn't being loud or anything to keep her awake—I was only striking the keyboard with my fingertips and loud thoughts.

"Whatever you are working on—can you stop it?" I was only halfway looking her way while I continued to complete a thought in my book. I stopped typing, did the squinty-eye thing and turned to look her way fully. Golda knew of the two topics that I was writing my books on at the time surrounding Jesus and angels. There was nothing that should have concerned her, so it puzzled me why she said this.

"I haven't been sleeping good at all, I keep having nightmares—like—really bad ones. So what are you working on?!" She was nearly demanding and I hadn't heard her

HEIDI HOLLIS

attribute her lack of sleep to anything I was doing before, so this was highly strange of her.

"I'm writing on my Jesus book right now." I replied.

"No that's not it, what else are you doing?" She asked firmly.

All I could think of that she may be hinting to was The Hat Man stuff I was finally trying to address. "Well, I did get in touch with these people who might help me figure out what's going on with The Hat Man—"

"That's it—can you stop it please?! I can't take this anymore!" She rubbed her head and face in frustration.

"Huh? Why do you think that has anything to do with you? What are your nightmares about?" I asked emphatically.

"Just trust me, that's what it is! So—promise me you will stop it? I really need to get some sleep. I've got too much to do for school and I can't risk this getting in the way—okay?" Golda got up and went to her room after I quietly said I would hold off on looking into it for now.

I don't know what surprised me more about what had just happened: Golda being as direct as she was—nearly demanding, or that darkness had effected someone other than myself because of my actions! It was a "HUH?" and a "WTH" moment if I'd ever had one before!

Golda was getting her Master's degree in business, which is no easy task in any part of the world, so I knew her stress level was high. But how did she know that I was looking into something darker than usual while I was writing my two books on something so positive?! She never did tell me what her nightmares involved, either.

Golda had already had her share of seeing the nightmare, Hat Man, in-person. So, I suppose not having to discuss anything related to darkness was pertinent to keeping her sanity while in school. I swear this is a typical scenario that I personally don't understand. So often I've run into people being reluctant to speak about something dark or paranormal, when so much could have been learned from their experience.

This is the typical story of my life!

Even you, the reader, can see how many times I've had to cut-off a story because someone wasn't willing to share something. Sometimes I can't help to wonder if something else didn't want them to share! It's a good thing that isn't the way I roll with my life in sharing more than enough—I guess ☺. But I wasn't always so forth coming, as you can also read in here.

As promised to Golda, I halted my looking into The Hat Man at that time, but it ate at my mind and soul. It worried me that he apparently intimidated and perhaps even threatened my friend in the form nightmares. I wondered what I had just gotten myself into. The power and nerve of this thing shocked and terrified me at the same time!

For the record, I did always intend to call Lorraine Warren. But apparently it wasn't meant to be ever. I shoved and tucked The Hat Man horror and hid what I was realizing in hopes he would somehow go away. I at least tried to forget him for the time being. Later, I again stepped forward to take a closer look at him through the stories I received and this time—he looked back at me!

7

HAT MAN PATTERNS:

It's In The Details

While I hung out in Australia, I got really comfortable with the idea of living there on a permanent basis. That's how much I had fallen in love with the country and the people who lived there. They have this number system there where they add up a tally of good assets that you have that can benefit Australia to accept you as a permanent resident. Luckily, the numbers were on my side (I thought I was an asset anyhow) and I was just about to set into motion the process of residency when a peculiar thing happened.

For as long as I can remember since I've been in this odd business of the supernatural, hyper-natural, para-natural, extra-natural stuff (I'm just making these words up as I go along—if you haven't noticed), there has always been a potential "television project" looming. Meaning, there was always someone who thought to contact me and try to get a new television series started with me involved in it somehow. After years of this chatter, I really stopped holding my breath for any of that to ever come through. Besides, having a television show wasn't why I got into these topics, so it wasn't a huge focus of mine.

Five months into my stay in Australia, I got two television show offers! Me still not believing any of it, I told myself, "I will believe it when they send me a contract." Well, against all odds, then one of the networks sent me a contract!

I was so set on staying in the Land of Oz, though! But it seemed there were other plans for me now—I had to come back to the United States! So, I waited to the very end of my six month-extended stay. Then I got a last-minute, one-way ticket back home to Wisconsin with only two days to spare on my Visa and left my Oz dream behind.

From a land of purple birds, killer land-birds, and bugs with opposing thumbs that were able to hold up my morning paper for me—back to post-Hurricane Katrina, United States! I had missed the majority of the horrific reports of hurricane-human neglect from the full perspective that was presented in the United States at the time. But the message was clear of how horrible man can treat one another. It was a dark time in American history and the air even seemed gray in color and mood, at times.

I had a lot of time to kill before filming would begin for my new show, so I thought to find a therapy position and move from my temporary stay at my parent's home. It was a first for me to come back home since moving out for college when I was 18 and I actually had a blast getting reacquainted with my parents and siblings. When I initially left for Oz, it was a near goodbye for an extremely long time and we celebrated it as such. Now I was back home and essentially had some more fun catching up about my adventure Down Under.

During our chats, it got mentioned how a sibling of mine had seen some Shadow Spiders in her room at night. Her boyfriend concurred about the many incidences that he had to react to her screaming in the middle of the night. Oddly or not so oddly, she didn't want to go into a whole lot of details with me, so the topic got skipped and skimmed over. Meanwhile, the stories kept pouring into me via email.

Dear Heidi,
This story starts when I was five years old. My mom had just sent me to bed, though I protested with all that I had. As I lay in bed, refusing to close my eyes, I looked at my bedroom door and saw something odd manifest. A bright red tunnel, with horizontal lines began to form and literally come out of the door! My room was completely black, except for the light coming from this red tunnel.

That's when I saw this man in black appear!

He came right out of the tunnel, wearing a black trench coat and top hat. He was walking towards me, but he wasn't actually getting any closer or gaining ground. I was completely filled with terror as I started screaming for my mom to come!

My mom came running into my room and I told her what I saw as fast as I could. I wasn't believed, of course. It wasn't until much later that I learned from my sister that she had seen this Hat Man, too. She claimed to have even had conversations with him, but she couldn't remember anything that was said. But my mom would always ask her who she was talking to and she would reply, "The man in the hat and coat."

My sister eventually moved away to college and she had a good friend who lived next door to her. One time in the middle of the night, her friend came banging on her door saying that a man in a top hat was sitting on her bed! My sister told me that she laughed and said, "He was probably just looking for me!"

My other sister said that her new boyfriend claimed that he saw The Hat Man standing right over him in bed as soon as she left the house! Tons of strange and bad luck has always been in my life. I've even had dreams of being in a dark place with Shadow Watchers and Shadow People in rooms with cages.

I believe that this Hat Man that's been visiting us is pure evil.

When it came to positive aliens, they often traveled through blue tunnels of light as was indicated in *The Secret War*. The only other time I heard of a red tunnel was when an evil entity took a child through a wall. That child described what sounded like an alien-human hybrid, who took her to a very hot and smelly place that smelled like rotten eggs (or sulfur) to her. What this person pointed out here as repeated dreams of "cages" in a dark place, is a vision of a Hell-like place that many people report seeing and literally experiencing. I referred to a similar incident in my other books *The Secret War* and *Jesus Is No Joke*. So many dark connections were being made in my mind while reading these emails, and they still are where I know I will one day need to continue to search.

As my stomach remained dropped in reading the messages I received then, I saw a pattern emerge that I had been trying to ignore for so long. The Hat Man screamed that he was not a shadowy Shadow Person—but that HE WAS SOLIDLY REAL!

I wasn't prepared to hear all that my gut had to say, but I continued to whittle down the details of differences I saw. I had already dropped the word "Shadow" when I described The Hat Man (instead of putting "Hat Man Shadow"), but I knew that more thought had to be lent to this horrific horror of a man.

From what I had observed, the Shadows or Shadow People didn't like to be spotted out very easily. They often were seen in people's peripheral vision and would seem to dodge out of the way quickly. This didn't happen for every scenario, but it was at least sometimes an initial encounter or at some point it occurred. But The Hat Man, when he came by he simply stood there or walked by and it didn't matter if you saw him cross-eyed—you could see him! People would see him at all times of day or night, outside or inside, raining or snowing! What's that motto the United States Postal Service has that no weather can stop them from delivering mail? Well, he's kind of like that!

I have been known to say that an enemy has the upper hand or "jump" on you if you don't know your enemy or see him coming. It was told to me by positive beings, that the Shadow People hid for this very reason—they wanted the upper hand. For instance, say that you personally wanted to sneak up on your friend to give them a miniature heart attack by suddenly screaming two inches from their ear. You would go into stealth mode then, right? You know—get your once clumsy feet into gear to lightly tiptoe, look to your left and right, estimate which floorboards squeaked, and avoid any obstacles that might get you caught before the grand execution of your scare tactic. Then, "ARRGH! I'm a mad Jedi—The Force betrayed me!" You blurt out, or whatever you want to scream out in fright.

That's when your friend quickly falls over in a faint! Mission accomplished then, right?

Now, with the same goal in mind to scare the crap out of your friend, you walk straight up to them this time. You lean in closely and scream about The Force betrayal, so forth and so on and wait for your friend to faint. More than likely he will just call you a freak and walk away and post about it on your

Facebook wall. So essentially, your approach made no sense to even attempt, right? I mean, how are you going to get the upper hand to scare them, encourage a fainting spell or bladder leakage for a good pants wetting with that level of effort?

Exactly. It makes no sense.

Shadow People go into stealth mode, gaining the element of surprise even though they are often getting caught as the veil between dimensions thins. The Hat Man doesn't even bother, he just shows up, mostly. While I was trying to figure out what was going on with this Hat Man guy, I thought he was awfully brazen, bold and ballsy—to say the least!

But truly, why would this Hat Man (or what I still thought might be a Shadow Person) do this? In thinking in the same scenario of wanting to scare my friend as much as possible—what if I approached my friend directly as The Hat Man does to his victims? Where I just walk straight up to them without saying a word and have the same effect as someone who put a ton of effort by going into stealth mode?

Well I'd say that I must be pretty bad-ass! I mean, if my presence alone could scare the crap out of my friend—that is truly an accomplishment to behold! Wouldn't you say?

Then I thought, "Hold on here, this guy wants to be seen! He even gets dressed for the occasion!"

Imagine:

If I were a particular Bigfoot tromping through the woods on any given starry night, I might get comfortable with my surroundings at some point to want to stay there in the area. Then, Bigfoot hunters across the country fly in and start tracking me and my lovely footprints down. Plaster casts are made of my foot impressions and the hunters go on record showing my foot casts talking about how typical my feet are to other casts made across the country.

One night, I catch the evening news (yeah—I'm a very informed Bigfoot ☺) and I hear they have called me and my prints "typical"! The nerve! So then I start to dress it up a bit and get a pedicure with a perfect shade of passion-purple polish. I buy a year's supply so I can keep the layers nice and thick. I do this just to be sure that every time I left a foot impression from now on, a flake of my favorite polish hits the dirt, too! That would then be my signature, my flare, my angle, my uniqueness to make these hunters tell my story in a new tone that the Bigfoot in these hills ruled it like no other!

In the beginning, this was the kind of reasoning I used in regard to The Hat Man, with a less silly angle—of course. He was a Shadow Person getting all fancied up and taking on a new form to show he had a plethora of forms he could take to show his versatility. Actually, I thought these new digs or clothes were exhibited to simply show the vast capabilities of the Shadow People and how they were not ones to be cornered or figured out. But I had already spelled out in *The Secret War* book, about their origins, goals and main habits.

Now I was realizing, that the particular clothing of The Hat Man was not shown to be very versatile. His hat seemed to change a little to being a fedora, to a gaucho hat, to even a top hat (or no hat—though less common). But no, he didn't change very much to show he had a diverse wardrobe. No—The Hat Man wore what he did to be recognized!

Even now when I write this, I get a lump in my throat of putrid horror in now realizing this.

To think, that this entity presented himself was ultimately done for recognition. That was just bone chilling! He was who he was, he is as he presents himself: A man in a dark suit, trench coat or cape, and a hat.

I would sometimes look at the image on my website of The Hat Man and ask it, "You want people to know who you are, to know your silhouette, your presence, your feel—but why?"

A mystery wasn't what he was trying to present, he was clear and his victims understood a lot more than they were always telling me in their emails. But, there came another pattern. People would write how they didn't understand why this Hat Man showed up and then would say how right before he showed, someone got sick. Then others would say how he showed up at the scene of an accident. Others noticed him coming around right after or before someone died.

Dear Heidi,

I have never been afraid of the dark. Not even as a kid, the dark never bothered me. I actually felt at ease in the dark, but now—I am terrified. I have had one encounter with a Shadow Person and it has changed my life ever since.

I was driving out to my friend Mark's house out in the country at 3 AM. I was on the phone with my fiancé when I pulled up into his driveway. I used my shoulder to hold the phone up to my ear so I could keep my hands free. That's when I glanced in my rearview mirror and saw a pitch-black figure dart by the back of my car.

Like I said, Mark lives out in the country so there are no other light sources besides the lamp they have near their walkway leading up to their house. But across the street, their neighbors have a small light above their garage. So when this figure passed behind my car it

blocked the light of the garage across the street. Since it was so distinctive, I knew for a fact that something passed by that was tall enough to fill the entirety of my rearview mirror!

Mark knew I was coming over, so I thought that it was him trying to sneak up on me to scare me. I turned around and looked out of all of my windows—but I didn't see anything!

"That's weird," I thought.

In the meantime, I am still on the phone talking to my fiancé and telling her that Mark is trying to scare me. I then opened the door to my car and felt a sudden rush of energy heading straight for me. I quickly lost my breath, so I slammed the door shut!

I told my fiancé I had to go and dropped the phone.

It was pitch-black outside, so I couldn't see any figure running for me—but I felt it. The energy, I might even say, the wind that it created—was REAL! I was totally freaked out.

I waited a minute or two, but I felt completely vulnerable and unsafe. It felt like something was behind me. Either it was behind the car or it was already in the car with me. Then I just jumped over the gearshift and into the passenger's seat and bolted out of the door heading straight for the house!

When I got inside I told Mark what had happened. That's when he reminded me of what he told me before about his house being haunted because of the cemetery on his land. He asked where I parked and experienced what I just told him of that odd energy. That's when he said that's the creepiest spot on his property.

Mark said that every time he was near that area that he could feel something watching him. The driver's side door of my car was literally feet from this pole that he said was the worst spot. I don't know if you have had any instances of Shadow People being tied to a location, Heidi, but this might be the case here. Needless, to say he told me about Shadow People and that's what he thought I had encountered. We got to talking and he told me about him and his family's other experiences—I stayed up all night because I was too scared to sleep:

Mark told me that he would wake up in the middle of the night and his bedroom door he always had shut, would be wide open. In the doorway, there would be a man standing there, wearing a hat (he said what looked like to be a cowboy hat) just staring at him. He says that this happened many-many times and this Hat Man never seemed to cross the threshold into his bedroom.

After he told me these stories I looked Shadow People up on the Internet and found the picture of The Hat Man and got goose bumps! When I found it, I told him about other people seeing this Hat Man and that he was called, "The Hat Man." Mark's exact words were, "You have to be f*cking kidding me!"

He then said that this entity had followed a couple of his girlfriend's home, after they encountered him at their residences. Heidi, have you heard of The Hat Man or Shadow People being able to follow people home once they have entered a home where they have been sighted?

The thing that REALLY creeps me the hell out is what happened to our friend Tim who left Mark's house late at night. While driving, Tim peeked in his rearview mirror and literally saw The Hat Man sitting behind him! Tim slammed on the brakes and turned to look fully behind him—but he was gone!

The strangest thing with this though, was that Tim slammed on his brakes and stopped only ten feet away from a fallen tree in the road. Had he not slammed on the brakes, he would have smashed right into it—no doubt! Tim feels that The Hat Man warned him about the tree, but he also said he felt ill will from him. Personally, I think The Hat Man was in the back seat waiting to watch the wreck and Tim just happened to look back. Crazy huh?

Another instance involved Mark's dad, Jim. Mark's family has had experiences with ghosts and other odd things their entire lives. Jim was never scared by any of it—until now. He was watching television in broad daylight, laying on the couch in the living room. He felt something watching him, so he looked over his shoulder and there was The Hat Man—only three feet away! Jim said his heart and breath both stopped and he could do nothing but stare. Neither he nor The Hat Man moved for about a minute, then The Hat Man turned and disappeared down the hallway in the direction of Jim's bedroom. Jim set the remote controller down and ran out of the house and didn't come back for three hours because of the sheer horror of the intrusion!

One more thing, I'm not even sure if it is related to Shadow People, but I thought I should mention it. Mark's bedroom is known to be the most haunted in the house. He says that he was lying in bed one night when all of the lights dimmed out. He said that there was moonlight coming through the window, and his bedroom was lit up by the glow of his computer screen. Light was seeping in through his closed door from lights still being on outside of his room.

Then all of a sudden, all of the lights dimmed out into pitch-blackness!

He says there was absolutely no light. Then there was a really loud and deep exploding bass note that

burned through his room. He says he put his hand in front of his face and he couldn't even see it. He screamed as loud as he could and couldn't even hear his own voice. He felt that he was somehow trapped in this dark void for what seemed like forever while he screamed out for his parents. I guess he knew that he was still in his room, because he could feel his furniture. Once he knew which way to go, he ran for the door.

When he opened the door and light poured in, he ran to his parent's bedroom. They were up watching television when he told them what happened. He asked them why they didn't come after him when he was screaming. They told him that they didn't hear anything and their bedroom is directly above his.

Gut instincts.

People were writing and showing me that they were able to link the connection about what made The Hat Man come near the one time, several times, or just once and never to return. People were also noticing places Hat Man liked to hang out at, like poles, cemeteries or just prior to an accident. Yes, these were all patterns. The people who only saw The Hat Man once seemed especially more able to link his appearance to something highly negative going on at the time. But when you are stuck in a void of a haunted area, triggers that might awaken The Hat Man to show up can become blurred.

It was clear that The Hat Man was begging to be noticed when he appeared, at times. Even if The Hat Man was simply walking by, or not expecting to be noticed by anyone. Even in those instances, it still seemed that once he sensed there was a person watching him he would often respond back with a stare of his own as noted in this story told to me by another friend of mine at a later time:

"While living in San Francisco when I was five years old and my sister was six, we saw something really strange one night. I don't know what brought our attention to look out of our bedroom window, but when we did we saw this strange looking man outside. He was going around the neighbor's house, looking in through their windows and just kept going around and around the house.

"That was weird enough, but what was really strange is that he looked like a man straight out of the 1800's with a long trench coat and top hat—all in black! We couldn't help but to stare at him a little bit to see what he was up to. But we couldn't make any sense of what he was doing.

"We had only seen him for a few moments when he suddenly turned quickly as if to stare right at us! Me and my sister screamed and pulled the curtains to hide that we were looking at him. But we only waited a couple of seconds before we decided to peek out again—somehow he got RIGHT UP TO OUR WINDOW!!!

"His face was SO horrifying to see!

"He had the most sinister grin across his face like the Joker out of Batman! He was older, like in his 60's and heavily wrinkled. We screamed and ran away from the window and told our mom. It was a good thing that she believed us and told us it was the devil so she said a prayer of protection to help keep him away!

"In thinking back on it all, the feeling of terror that came over us was unbelievable. But there was no doubt in our mind that this thing was real and he could move fast! Our neighbor's house was over 100 feet away and

**this Hat Man cleared it in mere moments to be right up
to our window!"**

As The Hat Man's habits became clearer and the people
who shared with me became more open—a dark veil seemed
to drop. The identity of this Hat Man was revealed and an
actual name came forward...

8

THE HAT MAN
UNCLOAKED:

Evil

E arly on, I got the rare email where the name of this Hat Man character was tossed around. This is when I first thought to not look any further so no one would ever have to hear me discuss the name. It was too dark and sinister to be real, besides. I also wanted to be sure this wasn't just randomness fluttering around in these few experiencer's minds.

While I was getting back to the normal routine of living back in the United States, it served to be a nice distraction. There was a lot to get used again and the biggest thing was rewiring my brain to know how to cross a street or drive on the right side of the road again versus the left side. It's surprisingly difficult to keep that sort of thing in mind, what once came so naturally. I then had to get used to the little things in life like the lack of shark and crocodile attack reports on television and fist-to-fist combats between people at odds with each other (handguns weren't allowed in Australia so they did things the old fashioned way). I of course was still mostly missing the vibrancy of Australia and its people. Yet there I sat, having to start working again after a long hiatus of writing and relaxing in the unique Land of Oz and its special creatures.

The emails continued to come in steadily about the Shadow People, who were unrelenting in their approaches to their victims. I would in fact say that they were the more aggressive ones in comparison to The Hat Man. I could easily refer to those unfortunate to have witnessed the Shadow People, as "victims." The Shadows loved to haunt, taunt and physically harass witnesses who were not always aware of their presence. However, that darn Hat Man didn't seem to have a need or desire to do much of that sort of thing with consistency.

No-no, The Hat Man came across as a "mob boss" type who didn't seem to want to get his suit wrinkled or dare to get his hands dirty (though not always of course). He mostly just gazed, stared or walked by a person in the midst of life and instilled a fear so rare—it remains there for an eternity!

What an interesting trick and specific ability to have.

Just as a mob boss could instill fear and respect with just his presence alone—was the same true for this Hat Man? Was there something preceding him when people met him where he was gaining respect from his unsuspecting witnesses? Should they have expected him? I was beginning to think that something else was going on, something else was getting emitted from this Hat Man and from his witnesses:

Dear Heidi,

I have read about the Shadow People on your websites and heard about your research. I want to tell you something that might really shock you!

What if I tell you that I have projected myself into the dimension where they live?!

It is VERY possible to go there and communicate with them. However, when it comes to The Hat Man be sure to steer clear of him! He is the meanest one, because he is not a Shadow—but the devil!!!

Now what gave this person that impression?

They say first impressions are lasting and can mean everything. So if we are to trust that notion when we are met with a new person—what is this revelation going on here with The Hat Man? What is bubbling up in people to say "Devil" out of all the names that could be tossed around?

I have heard the vague term of "ghost" being attributed when a person is met with a partially seen apparition of a person who may have lived once. Sometimes people are lucky enough to maybe even find out who died in the certain place that the "ghost" was spotted and find the name to the exact spirit seen. There's an apparent link that way; you see a ghost that looks like the previous homeowner and you have a plausible cause to what's going on.

So, I wondered if the people who wrote to tell me these particular stories and used the name "devil," if it just fit the definition for them personally. Perhaps they had a preconceived idea that the devil preferred to wear black trench coats and suits, for all that I knew. But still, for them to even fathom that they themselves had just met the devil had to be a hard conclusion to come to and even admit!

So, I still questioned how people came to the conclusion that they did and why they would dare even go there to say this devil name. I have already carried on in telling of our gut instincts and such, but still something else was at work here. I think that often when we are knowingly about to meet someone, a reputation precedes us before we interact. So, you will most definitely have expectations:

Let's say Kayden is known to be a "butthead." Meaning, Kayden doesn't listen to anyone giving him advice or insight about anything. In fact, Kayden is a terrible listener and everyone knows it. He dresses like a bum, mocks people, is spoiled rotten, but you are his godfather and he's looking for a job at the place where you are the boss!

You hadn't seen him in a while and his family has put the pressure on you to take him in and interview him for a position. The image in your memory of what he's like burns in your mind and your stomach quakes at the thought of letting him anywhere near your company that you run so darn well.

Kayden comes in, dressed for nothing successful, does a half-bear man hug, shows himself to your office and your leather chair and puts his feet up on your desk with clumps of mud landing on your computer keyboard! You know inertly that nothing fruitful will become of this job interview as you succumb to sitting in the other seat and ask Kayden what his goals are for working at your company. Then you see his ear buds are in listening to his favorite tunes, so he doesn't even hear you ask anything.

This was all to be expected, because this is who Kayden is, whom we all know and still love.

In today's society, we all have seen a glimpse of a horror movie or two. The evil entity or devil dresses in some dark threads and may even sport some retractable horns atop of his head with a sly smile to match. He generally is depicted as a man, or even a man-beast who has the ability to transform into something more acceptable by human standards. Then there's the devil depicted who can turn into a loin-cloth wearing, horned beast with blazing red eyes or black ovals. The devil is *known* and he is always depicted as being an interchangeable and forever evasive creature.

The Hat Man enters—and he just happens to fit the criteria embedded in the minds of the witnesses to him so they call him "devil?" I thought this was a possibility, anyhow.

Had this been what was going on with this attributed devil name with The Hat Man? I had to wonder. Were people only assuming things because of what they were seeing? Were they feeling so fearful because he looked a certain way? Then a reversal of thought came my way. I wondered if The Hat Man was the one who was actually emitting the fear inspirations filled with respect, fully on his own. But I still struggled and felt that mostly it was the fearful respect that was being given to him through assumptions and kneejerk reactions by witnesses.

So many questions rolled and fumbled in my head. Then things got interesting. The Hat Man started to speak more clearly:

Dear Heidi,
I was stationed in Germany and I had the nightshift for guard duty. I thought I was running late because I missed my alarm clock. So I woke up startled and started rushing around getting my uniform on as fast as I could. After that, I ran into the bathroom to shave when I thought I saw someone walk by the doorway.
No civilians were allowed in the barracks where we were all housed and the barracks were pretty empty

since most of the guys were out doing an overnight exercise. So I looked to see if I could spot the civilian I thought I saw, but no one was down the hallway in either direction. I had to get ready quickly, so I went back to the sink to rinse out my shaver.

When I went to look up, I saw the reflection of this man in a black-rimmed hat and trench coat—standing behind me! I asked him, "Who are you? How'd you get in here?"

As he tipped his hat as if to introduce himself, he said, "I'm Scratch."

I then turned around to see him directly, but he was gone!

Then I rolled out of my bed unto the floor! I'd never gotten out of bed?! Had it all only been a dream? It didn't seem like it and it felt as real as anything! I was SO shaken up by this experience that it bothered me enough to do some research on this name "Scratch."

I later found out that "Old Scratch" is a Norse term for "the devil!"

It felt like I had met pure evil and he introduced himself as such!

Another story that threw me was one told to me some time ago, or written to me via someone whose email I can no longer find. But the story remains distinctive in my mind. This person was in the basement of their home, the lights were dim when suddenly The Hat Man appeared next to them. The Hat Man quickly pointed to the wall and they were shocked to see a scene appear, much like a movie screen.

It looked like a torrential storm upon a rocky ocean of water! There in the middle of it was a ship that was obviously in trouble. On the deck of the ship, stood a man who didn't seem to even try to save himself from his doomed ship. The witness then watched in horror as the ship went down into the dark waters with the man secure on his dark destiny to the bottom of the sea.

The person was then rocked to look back at The Hat Man when he said, "Such a man would do this for me!" He then vanished in an instant!

To ask that someone die for this Hat Man, took the nerve of something far more horrifying than I cared to imagine. What are we facing here? What has turned its hideous head to look our way and stake its claim to say such things to people? Why now, here, and one person at a time?

Do you see now why I wished I hadn't looked any further, at times?

9

EYE OPENERS:

Closing My Eyes

All that I had suspected with people potentially assuming the wrong things about this Hat Man—were wrong! The Hat Man was in charge of inspiring what people thought and they titled him accordingly and properly. Another point about this is—The Hat Man knew exactly how he was being perceived and he wanted to be known as such. Then apparently if people asked or weren't sure who he was, he just might share his name.

Are you getting the chills yet, or is it just me?

This freaking Hat Man was and is the devil?! What kind of clean up in one's mind needs to take place once that nuclear bomb of spiritual warfare goes off? For me, it was messy!

It was hard for me to take in this reality and each of these people who were writing me thought that they were the only ones to have seen him until they came across my website! So at this point, these people who were writing me, they hadn't discussed their experiences with anyone else to compare notes or ideas. Yet against all odds, these people were coming to the SAME conclusions and answering their own questions with: "Who is he? He's the devil isn't he?"

Would you believe, but I once was a skeptic of there even being a devil?!

I even used to heavily question another phenomenon that was the polar-opposite of The Hat Man. I simply just did not believe in holy encounters with Jesus that are often being reported worldwide. I have personally seen and experienced a lot of supernatural things in my time. In fact, I have actually bore witness to seeing several angels and angelic-like beings. The angelic types who looked closer to being human, often wore long white robes, but sadly had no wings to be seen.

I was so sure of myself and of the things that I had experienced (because we all do know and trust our own instincts above anyone else's—right?) that I doubted reported sightings of Jesus. I know how idiotic that sounds of me to have felt so strongly in opposition, but I did! I was absolutely positive that people were mistaking angels for Jesus! I felt that what they saw must have fit the assumptions and stereotypes of Jesus. I was sure that they must have seen a male angel wearing a long-white robe, giving off a strong feeling of love, coming in a time of need and perhaps even having some flowing, shoulder length hair!

Well I had seen all of those things in the angel types that I had witnessed and I *knew* they weren't Jesus. I also knew that my senses didn't tell me to kneel, bow, or change my whole perspective on life because of who I was seeing. You see, I allowed my assumptions of what a Jesus encounter would entail. So I expected at least a moment of being blown away in awe, if I had seen Jesus.

Life is so funny, though. Because I did actually get my chance later, when I met Jesus four times!

Oh—and I didn't just bow, kneel or change my life's perspective, either. Nope! I back flipped in excitement, changed my **everything** in life, was healed of an incurable disease and wrote about it my book *Jesus Is No Joke* and am now forever in awe of what took place in this onetime skeptic's life!

So in now looking back on my experiences with Jesus, I recall how immediate the recognition was that I had of Him. I had only for a split second allowed my eyes to try to place a label on who I was seeing, but it was not a lasting thought. I have gone on record to say and will forever say that I could have been blind and seen it was Jesus! Every cell in my body screamed His Name and of that I have **no doubt**.

The question is; would seeing something equivalent to the devil be as recognizable?

I realize that the power of good is considered to reign over the powers of darkness, but it is a formidable enemy. In the eyes of the church and Christians, the main enemy of God is the devil, lucifer and satan (capital lettering is purposefully omitted—I give no respect to darkness even with capitalization ☺). So, if this is the most formidable force to even dare try to oppose God, then there is the good (no pun intended) chance that this punk gives off a "knowing" vibe of who he is, too!

If even there is this slight chance that The Hat Man has this powerful of a presence—this guy is dropping hints in various ways! He doesn't answer all riddles given to him and he doesn't want to. He doesn't tell people why he is there and he doesn't seem to have to. He doesn't have to be visible, but he wants to. He doesn't come back to everyone more than once and he might not be able to or he already left the impression he wanted in one visit.

There's still a lot to know about him and the only one true way to build up a case against him is we have to do it like they do in a court of law. That means that we have to find as many witnesses to the act of him being The Hat Man and let the jury (or you the reader) decide who he is and what his motives are by looking at the evidence presented to you.

First things first, the stories presented to you need to be taken with all of your precautions thrown in the wind. Okay that's too subjective, so I will take that back. Instead, I want you to be the judge, jury and prosecutor in the case for The Hat Man. I doubt anyone will want to defend a known horror inflictor, so there's no defense attorney in his case. Maybe there's some who would want a defense portrayed here, but unless you practice satanism I don't think it will be needed.

So, let the stories cometh forth and hither, for all to see!

I'm going to go through the thousands of emails here and see what may indeed help us all take a crack at reading between The Hat Man's dark threads to see what he is revealing.

Dear Heidi,

Thank you for your site.

When I was just 17 years old, I was 8 months pregnant. One night I listened in as my parents were chatting back and forth about something. My dad kept asking my mom what was wrong and my mom just kept saying that she was freezing. That was weird because it was a hot summer's night. So my dad didn't let up and kept bugging her until she finally said that she felt "Death" in the house!

About two weeks later, I was sleeping in my bed when I suddenly felt a chill that woke me up.

When I rolled over in bed with my eyes open, I saw a very black shadow of a man, with what appeared to be a

top hat on his head! He also was carrying a cane and he had a long coat with coattails on it. I couldn't make out any details of his body or face, just this shadowy figure of a man standing there.

After I saw him, I turned back over onto my other side. I tried to convince myself that I was imagining what I had just seen. Then suddenly it got bone chilling cold! I rolled back over and he was now directly to the side of my bed hovering directly above me!

As I looked at him he kind of lost his distinctive form. Then I felt like he was suddenly on top of me—choking me! I was quickly rendered unable to scream or move! So I did all that I could do. In my head I asked God, if He existed, to help me and to not let this thing kill me and my unborn child!

In that moment—it left!

It took me a few minutes to gather the strength to practically crawl over to my parent's bedroom. I was so weak and scared that it took a lot out of me to get there. I didn't hesitate in telling my parents that something had just tried to kill me. My mom said that I was being ridiculous because she thought if someone had come into the house she would have heard them. That's when I told her that it was not "someone," but "something" that had tried to kill me!

The next night, the Shadow Man was back in my room at the end of my bed. But this time, I could hear a clearly sinister laugh coming from him! That was it for me. I never wanted to be back and sleeping in my room ever again! I asked my parents if we could switch bedrooms the next night. I was happy that they agreed, because they got a sense that something was wrong in there because neither of them could sleep the whole night.

So next day my whole family gathered in my bedroom and we began to pray. My father prayed to God and said that we should not have to fear being in our own house. Then my dad bellowed, "Satan get out of here!" It did not even sound like my dad at that moment. Then suddenly we all saw this Shadow leave my bedroom— right through the window!

I never saw him again, but I never forgot him either.

Ah. The power that can be wielded once a group of people come together against evil—it's immeasurable! Had this girl sat alone in her own misery and knowledge in knowing what it's like to be in the presence of pure evil, she and her child may have never been here to share their story. Nor would she have ever had a chance to get help had she not called on the Power of God during her first encounter.

I'm actually impressed how she was able to convince her parents to switch bedrooms because of something like this happening. I don't think my parents would ever swap rooms for any reason I could ever think of. When it comes to these odd encounters, most times people need to see and experience things for themselves in order to be moved to act. I'm hoping that won't be the case one day, because evil is so thick and floating abound; people have got to realize that they are bound to run into it one day.

I always like to say that I am no more of an expert than the next person, but I feel I do know what I'm doing most of the time, anyhow. I'm sure that most of us feel rather confident in our own ways to decipher what enters within our own visual field. That old homage of "my eyes playing tricks on me" just doesn't add up always. Do you know how many times I've been told that by people who have told me their stories, that they "thought" it was their eyes that were up to no good?

These same people can be truck drivers who carry loads of goods from one coast to the other, but suddenly, their eyes just don't know how to relay a visual message? I don't recall these people indicating that because of this sudden vision problem that they submitted themselves to testing their eyes or taking a mental capacity test to determine their ability to decipher what they see. Nope. Instead, they just sat quietly with their tricky eyes until they thought perhaps their eyes weren't the sneaky devils (pun intended) they once assumed them to be.

It's kind of funny, isn't it?

Then there are the people who have not trusted their guts or other people's guts, for that matter. Some people who have seen my website and now other websites on The Hat Man that talk about his rotten ways—are raising all sorts of doubts about what's being experienced out there. I have had a small number of people tell me that they have personally seen The Hat Man several times and they don't feel anything evil about him. In fact, some have called him a guardian angel of a sort!

Now I really don't like to bash people for their beliefs, because who am I to judge with all of my otherworldly experiences? But I KNOW my experiences to be real for me and some people KNOW what they KNOW—right? And then, another pattern emerges:

Dear Heidi,

Would you believe that my very first encounter with The Hat Man happened when I was only a few months old? My two uncles were sitting on the sofa next to my mom while she was changing my diaper on the ottoman. That's when my mom said she noticed that I suddenly

stopped squirming and the expression on my face changed dramatically.

So she stopped what she was doing and looked over at her brothers to see what they were doing to make me react as I was. When she looked up at them, they were both slack jawed and pale while staring at something behind her. She quickly turned to see what they were looking at only to see The Hat Man looming over her!

As soon as she saw him—he disappeared.

While growing up, I saw him a few more times. He would just usually show up in the doorway to my bedroom. My mom saw him when I was a teenager; he was just pacing back and forth in the hallway right in front of my bedroom. That's when he actually felt evil. My mom would have to start praying and just charge him to go right through him to get to me! When she did, he would just vaporize!

As I got older, The Hat Man didn't come around anymore. When we came across your website, my mom really freaked out. We always thought he was a guardian angel or something.

It has been few and far between, where I've heard from people who have considered these Hat Man encounters to be potentially something good. There has even been the person who, as I mentioned, doesn't believe that others have seen the true nature of The Hat Man. These people feel that these other witnesses who report The Hat Man as being negative, didn't actually get to know The Hat Man. Like they should have taken Hat Man's hand and snuggled or something? Okay, so I'm just kidding. But as with any topic, there will always be the person who thinks out of a million, their single perspective is correct. This story above, they weren't certain what to think of this Hat Man, but they did sense he was evil or at least "protective." So I wouldn't lump them in as being ones who thought he was fully positive since the mom did know to use prayer to confront this thing.

The pattern I'm seeing with other "Hat Man fans" is a different one. Some witnesses seem to get a boost in their ego that since they personally weren't scared whenever they saw The Hat Man, then that means The Hat Man *isn't* evil. More often it actually seems that those who have experienced The Hat Man more than once without fear, seem to be more at ease with his presence. They almost seem to feel connected to him, that his gaze is a watchful one and protective. Some even give him credit for helping them out in a given situation.

Dear Heidi,

I grew up with a physically abusive father who made me feel utterly helpless often times while growing up. Then the guy who you call The Hat man started showing up around the house when I was a teenager. I at first didn't know what I was looking at, because he seemed to almost blend in with the dark corners of the rooms he was in. We lived in a big house with poor lighting, so he had a lot of places to stare out at me from.

Then he just started sitting on the couch or the edge of my bed and would just stare at me directly. I was so miserable as a kid as it was, that his presence more like puzzled me than scared me. The Hat Man never seemed to be far, it's like I could feel his presence and his eyes on me all the time.

One day, my father got drunk and was sitting on the recliner when he got angry with me over something. I knew what that meant, that he was going to come after me to punch me. When he got off his chair to come swing

at me, The Hat Man just came out of nowhere and threw my dad backwards over the couch!

I was stunned as I watched this happen and The Hat Man quickly disappeared right afterwards!

My dad was so drunk he didn't know what hit him, but it stopped him from coming after me. I don't know what this Hat Man is, but he at least helped me out one time. I haven't seen him since I moved out of that house, but sometimes I wonder if he will ever come back.

When I first wrote and spoke on the more negative aliens (the abducting aliens), I shared how they often took advantage of their victim's trusting nature. The abducting aliens would, at times, heal their victims and even give their victims the "gift of healing." Though in actuality, it was the aliens working on people in the background. So when this new abductee healer would put their hands on someone to help heal them, these healers would admit to seeing their alien abductors working alongside of them to heal another person.

The old saying holds true, that we don't get "something for nothing."

They are not doing this out of the goodness of their hearts—these beings have no emotions. So they are indeed making sure that every time a favor is accepted from them, a debt is owed. These aliens are also sure to implant a leash on the soul of the person submitting to their kind of healing, as well.

I have a good friend who watched some testimonial videos and did some reading on a website that promoted healing to be done by alien beings. However, in order for you to receive your healing you would essentially have to internally and externally state how the aliens had permission to come to you for your healing performed by them. When I heard of this, I was more than appalled by the encouraged invitation of the "vampires of the universe" to come into a person's personal space and life!

So as soon as I explained to my friend how this may be, in fact, inviting something compared to the ranks of demons, he quickly said out loud, "I take it back!"

Sadly though, it would seem that it was too late to "take it back." A short time later, my friend said he awoke in the middle of the night because he sensed something was watching him. He quickly opened his eyes and saw something astonishing. Just merely inches from his face—he saw an alien face!

"As I looked at it, I couldn't believe my eyes and what I was seeing. Then suddenly, this thing seemed to be wondering if I could see him or not. I said to it, using my mind, 'Yes I see you!' Then it seemed shocked and quickly started to fade away into nothing!"

Scary! Mere words of saying that you will allow a being to come into you and it comes along so quickly to stake its claim!

The Hat Man is doing no less and much-much worse.

His presence isn't one to welcome. Especially when 99.9% of the percent of people who witness him report of only horror, the odds are that he is horrible. To compare yet again, some alien abductees will attest that THEIR personal, abducting aliens were the good guys. Yes, their aliens looked just like the rotten ones who did the same horrible things as others did, but to these abductees, these aliens were familiar where they even felt love for them.

Hat Man fan-witnesses, say the same thing: Hat Man does that same gawking-staring thing and he looks like the other reports of him. But his fans have written saying, "I like knowing he's nearby watching." Yet and still, these fans will sometimes say there have been some instances where The

Hat Man has caught them off-guard and scared the crap out of them. Sometimes he's even felt malevolent or aggressive towards them, but not always.

Ah, I shall always love using that word "crap!" But, I digress.

Dear Heidi,

Until this afternoon, I thought my seeing the very large shadow of a very large man in a fedora hat, was my unique experience!

He has been coming around me since I was a young kid, but I really didn't pay much attention to him. I lived in my own little world and he wasn't invited. But I felt that he checked in on me at times.

Then in my 20's he started showing up a lot.

I had just started my first fall into love with who I thought was a wonderful guy. After a year of being together, he suddenly went back with his ex-girlfriend and became quickly engaged. I was more than crushed.

Not long after the break-up, he started calling me frantically, but I didn't want to talk with him. When I finally decided to speak with him, he asked me an odd question. "Did you send your guy to my place?"

I didn't exactly know right away what he was talking about until he told me what happened. He said that his new fiancé literally bumped into The Hat Man in the kitchen! When she ran out to go get him, he came into the kitchen and also saw The Hat Man still standing there! I told him I of course didn't send him to go get them or anything.

I didn't feel badly for him, but I asked him what it felt like to see him. He said that he was more than frightened. I didn't think that I'd sent The Hat Man over there to harass them, he did this on his own for some reason.

Oddly enough, The Hat Man scared the new fiancé out of town and the boyfriend right back into my life! Though I had seen who my boyfriend really was and didn't like that view either—I allowed him back in.

I've never had a 'fear' of Mr. Fedora, just a mild curiosity. That was just my personal feeling. This feeling was also encouraged by an inner "knowing" that he could not be close to me and that he really wasn't allowed to touch me physically.

Then one afternoon while I napped—he showed up!

I was having a bad dream or something and he shot over to the side of my bed! Then he placed his huge hand over mine, as if to comfort me. This was disconcerting on many levels, but my 'spirit' reacted first! I felt my spirit literally sit up, out of my body, and shake a finger at him—screaming, "You're not allowed to touch me!"

To this day I don't know why he wasn't allowed to touch me, only that it had a consequence for him. Whatever that means. But, that is when I decided he wasn't supposed to be around me.

After my spirit yelled at him, he shrank back. Then my spirit laid back down inside of me—thankfully!

Then when I looked again towards the foot of my bed, I saw what looked like the freaking Grim Reaper! He waved that thing he carries called a scythe in front of him. Then my Grandmother's admonition to 'stand up and rebuke' evil things, sprang again into my mind. That's when my spirit got really pissed off and banished the both of them!

I was truly amazed by my spirit to have taken the battle on the way it did. Then I woke up and called out to my grandmother. She tried to comfort me, but then told me, "He will come back." And he did, a lot!

But my grandmother also said, "Don't give him any emotion—nothing!"

I am older now and he still shows up! Usually, I get a voice in my head from him saying, "I have been with you forever—no harm from me." I still send him back to Hell, with a little thought and a big prayer!

Just now realizing that I'm not alone, in a global sense, has totally sent me into orbit! And as I write this, Mr. Fedora is just out of sight, when I think about him he's there. He doesn't get in, but he's tricky.

I always had a sense that he was 'concerned' about me and I still have that sense. But Grandma told me, "It's what they do." I asked her if he could be my guardian angel? Then she asked me what did it feel like when he was near and the gut said, "This isn't right."

My cat didn't even like him. She would hiss and make a big fuss and she was only a four-pound, little Persian. She often woke me up with her little hissing party, so I knew he had been there.

This Shadow Man is slick, but he never had a chance with my Grandma on my side. Grandma was a 'prayer warrior' like no other! She shared with me a long time ago to gird myself in the armor of God. I did, do, and always will!

I'm very spiritual and awhile back I did a little ritual to make The Hat Man go away. Now after a super long time, he's back and this started only a couple of months ago! I've always had the 'dreams' you describe. But with my armor newly shined—we fight the fight! Again though, I know he is attracted by emotion and my mother passed a few months ago, so he saw a chance to make his move apparently.

Mr. Fedora is a phantom. He's got nothing to gain if you turn off the fear and passion and instead rile them up into a prayer of conviction! There are natural laws about this situation with The Hat Man. Maybe one day I will know what the consequence is that he will get if he touched me that I felt so strongly about, it will always fascinate me.

I am really blown away by this, Heidi! You have blown a lid off this and I have a feeling I better get out all of my armor—I'm going to need it!

-Thanks!

So, why would The Hat Man seemingly protect and at other times not? Perhaps the perception is wrong here. Maybe what is being witnessed isn't being done to be helpful at all. As seen in this story, there was a looming consequence felt in there somewhere. Not only was a consequence felt that The Hat Man wasn't supposed to touch this person, but also the fact that The Hat Man didn't come alone-this was a dark twist. Here was this Grim Reaper type being, lurking there all the while Hat Man "comforted" this person. This Grim Reaper being is really starting to get involved a lot in the dark games around out there. I wonder what might have happened if this witness allowed his comforting to continue. Would the Grim Reaper gather up their soul? It came for a reason and I doubt it came to watch the love flow between The Hat Man and this witness.

What I really love about this story is how the spirit of this person was on alert and did what it internally knew to do to get rid of both of these evil things. It's amazing how somehow, in the midst of their darkest hour, these witnesses just throw their hearts to God. Then here's the soul of a person springing up to banish demonic forces like a well-versed exorcist! Just—amazing!

I'm also thinking that The Hat Man did his best to possibly try to reassure this person so that they wouldn't be steered away from him. When The Hat Man comes around again and again, I think he knows his grip on the person is weak. Like here he literally is suggesting, "No harm from me." Saying like it's okay because he's an old friend or something?!

Let's say I had a friend that I really wanted to understand where I'm coming from. Perhaps, I may even have a point that I really wanted this friend to know and it was of utmost importance that they do. So I tell them about it with all that I had. If my friend really "gets me" and can relate to me, I won't have to repeat myself. But say that I do keep repeating myself to them and lurk around trying to drive my point home? I'd probably come off as being insecure and my friend would come off as not really having that much in common with me to get what I'm trying to tell them.

Wouldn't you say?

Just so you know, in playing judge, jury and prosecutor, we are all allowed to speculate—including me. So, I'm just speculating about the possibilities here and I think it's healthy that I do so. Because, if we are indeed speaking about the devil here, is there really no area of the evil spectrum that I cannot roam and conjure up any possible motives?

Yeah, I didn't think so either...

10

NECESSITY:

Becoming An Informant

I didn't want to look...
  I had already known and realized what I was dealing with during that first year in 2001 when I got my first handful of emails regarding that Hat Man drawing. But who in their right mind wanted to cover stories about the devil himself? It was nothing I was eager to get involved with, but every so often my mind would lean towards the necessity of my speaking up.

I thought of ways I should go about it, but it seemed when I did, the victims of his presence were brought closer to him. Those closest to me also seemed to get an extra dose of negativity spewed their way, but it couldn't be an eternity before I would share my findings. As the letters kept pouring in, I actually started to feel anger towards the phenomenon and Hat Man's ability to come and go with no one but myself connecting how widespread his appearances were. I was so much more willing to go towards more positive topics like the Jesus encounters, even positive alien contact. But it kept nagging at me and burning in me to open my mouth and do a tell-all on Coast to Coast Am with George Noory in 2006.

I couldn't bite my tongue any longer and with the airing of my interview, the number of emails focusing only on The Hat Man came in shocking numbers! Not only were there more emails, but they also became more lengthy and detailed stories. I had my work cut out for me, to say the least, and it was only me trying to handle it all.

Experiencers started chatting amongst themselves online in forums talking about Hat Man and what had happened to them and the effects on their lives The Hat Man had created. With knowledge comes power, in numbers comes strength, and with communication comes answers. The ball got rolling on the phenomenon that was spotted randomly by witnesses. Now they all had a name to do a search online for that topic where it could hopefully produce some results for them personally—"The Hat Man."

This new trend also brought shocking results to me on a personal level. I realized that if I hadn't spoken up, that many people would have felt alone and never realized who and what they had met. What a horrible reality to live in, feeling that you just met the premiere "evil doer" in your bedroom the night before and not have one single soul in the world who could relate to you?

I believe it's one of the cruelest realities to live in to feel that your soul is at risk.

We can say that we survived a car crash, a rape, a near death experience, and so on—because there is evidence to say that those things did happen to a provable extent. All of these things are extremely devastating to have been through, where they can change who you are. On top of it all, people understand what you have been through and are there to help and support you through your struggle in dealing with it.

Now, come shaking to your close friends and family and tell them on wobbly knees how you believe you may have just witnessed seeing the devil or something close to it walk out of your closet last night! Go ahead—even try to imagine it. I know I've been driving the point home on how the supernatural is nothing "super" and can feel "unnatural" and can be isolating. But the single element of fear of being ridiculed has left all of us not knowing—for all these years—that this Hat Man has been appearing all along to tons of people worldwide!

See my point yet or am I just getting hyped for nothing? ☺

I was super overdue in speaking out about this Hat Man guy, and I sincerely apologize for the delay. When I think of how alone I felt in experiencing all that I have, I know what it's been like for people wanting to find even a shred of camaraderie out there. I did do my best to individually answer the emails that came to me. I tried to lend some advice where I could to maybe help with the shared situations through my Alien Advice site, column and YouTube Channel. But I knew that more would need to be done.

I had shared with a handful of friends about the influx of Hat Man stories, especially after I went on-air discussing it. I knew and my friends knew that I would need to write another book to be specifically focused on this Hat Man irritant. But does anyone know what procrastination is? Please raise your hand and speak loudly if you have ever been afflicted with it.

It wasn't all about holding off on speaking about him because it gave nightmares to those close to me—life also got in the way. Yes, I also didn't like the idea of focusing so much on the devil, either, as I'd already mentioned. But I'm not going to bore you with the details on all of that any further—but timing is everything.

My life, livelihood, mental and physical capabilities had been threatened over and over again these past three years from May of 2011 to May of 2014—which is right now! Though it wasn't much appreciated having a ton of health issues happen to me, it gave me ample time to write as I recovered! Though I had more difficulty with my concentration, I was quite determined to get my books done that I had in mind.

Here's another participatory activity coming, class:

Raise your hand if you know someone who was diagnosed with a brain tumor, a spinal tumor, a brain aneurysm and a broken neck—all within six months?! The worst of these I am still dealing with. Talk about being a miracle to even be alive or of (partially) sound mind ever again! Well, all of that will be included in another book I feel that I have to write soon in continuing on Jesus' interventions in my life. Just when you think the devil has the strongest grip—Jesus rolls a bowling ball down the alley and knocks the devil into the gutter!

So when the thought and real possibility arose that I may not even be capable of, or even alive to write ever again came into my reality repeatedly, I thought, "Time to get off your backside, Heidi!" Ironically, it is indeed my backside I am forced to sit on in order to be writing this book now and it is going numb currently—no lie! ☺

It's a shame that it had to come to this for me to find the time and make the effort to finish my projects in the midst of such personal and emotional turmoil in the face of my own health crisis. While sitting in the Intensive Care Unit and being told of my nearly certain death, I thought of what I would want to live for. We all know how the cycle of life goes with the physical death of our loved ones being an awful process that we all have to go through and deal with. So, in thinking about my family and friends having to deal with the real possibility of my croaking right then and there—I honestly thought that they would get over it.

God help me when my friends and family read that last sentence, because I know that I'm going to be slammed with an onslaught of any one of these following statements:

a. "Huh?!"

b. "Are you freaking kidding me?!"

c. "WTH?"

d. "How could you say that bull-shizzle?!"

e. "I would have conjured your spirit up in a séance just to yell at you for even thinking that at any point!"

But what actually did come to my mind in my ICU bed as being most urgent was, "I need to live to finish the books I'm supposed to do!"

I started writing this book in 2004 and there it sat all of this time. Then one day, my mortality was splayed before my eyes then suddenly I'm halfway done writing this book in a months' time! Inspiration comes in strange ways, but they do indeed come at some point at least.

The good news is, I'm writing and I think I'm making some kind of sense here mostly.

I have wondered if it was in the cards for me to ever have a clear thought again at times, and that part is actually a fluctuating struggle. Partly being that I was a bit pre-occupied planning my next health intervention to take care of the next dilemma and the damage that I had going on in general. The thought did cross my mind that all of these strange and rare medical conditions all *had to* have some darkness behind it. I had been talking to friends about getting on top of my writings, especially with The Hat Man book as a top priority—then wham—rare brain tumor!

I had to find a way to get back on my game, but it was all doom and gloom being tossed around my diagnosis and prognosis. So I had little way of making a path in my mind through the rubble of destruction to see how I could ever write anything again. The rubble was mostly emotional and medical time-consuming stuff, though after my neck injury the pain was astronomical. My ability to speak clearly and concentrate to even think long had its challenges, too. All of this going on at once-was the boss of me and my daily life and focus. For anyone out there who has been through a health crisis or knows someone who has, I'm sure that you know what I'm speaking of here.

Every week I seemed to have another doctor appointment, scan, test, or belly ache in even thinking how I had to go see another doctor! It's kind of hard to hold down a job when you are needing to save your life and vitality. I had a hard time even doing my little bit of paperwork before me as I continued to practice as an occupational therapist. I had never ever been so far behind in all of my paperwork before, but at times the best I could do was sit there and stare at it. It was such a strange place to be in, but I had so little ability to focus my thoughts towards much more than a conversation. Even when I sat to watch television, the thoughts in my head on my health were louder than I could turn the volume up.

So, now I sit here still in one piece and on a mission of putting forward what I have seen and learned in hopes it doesn't end here. In fact, during my time as a radio talk show host on *Heidi Hollis-The Outlander* (on CBS Radio and

Inception Radio Network) and also *The Kevin Cook Show*, I helped organize a new group I called Paranormal Pledge. I first created it as a Facebook group and I always had the domain name sitting on-hold, but www.ParanormalPledge. com is now alive.

With Paranormal Pledge, I ask people who have written me or that I've helped, or anyone who has a curiosity or story to share about the paranormal—to raise their right hand and promise to tell one other person about it! This means that you don't sit on what you have experienced, been interested in or discovered in connection with anything out of the ordinary. Don't do what I did and sit around too long, in other words. Also, don't just sit online and search for answers secretly or just send a stranger like me your story! Tell others—tell the truth—share the knowledge now and not later! It simply is something that needs to be done.

Enough about me and this "mission" of sorts, but so you know, I don't plan on going anywhere anytime soon. Yet, God's plan is never one I can predict. In the meantime, back to what I'm here for:

People started to share their stories and find answers among themselves and it was and is a beautiful thing. Yet, in being human we can often find too much fault in others and look for someone else who will gather things together and tell them, "This is how it is and how I want you to perceive the truth!"

I don't really feel like doing that, but if it helps someone out there who would like to see some conclusions drawn, some lines crossed, some frayed responses, some heads-butted, some beliefs dropped, some bombs ignited, some cataclysm revealed, some seas parted, some peanut butter spread or some ice-cream scooped (yes-I'm digressing again), then I'm your girl (or lady, or friend, or gawker into the unknown)!

I'm charged up at full throttle and I want to let you in on a little secret—I have no idea on what I'm going to focus on next...

Okay—I just got an idea, now turn the page ☺!

11

HAT MAN HISTORY:

Nothing New

It's always said that there is nothing new under the Sun that it just goes by a different definition with our new words to say that we know better now. Evil has been written of for eons and the many forms it might come in. There are rules and definitions we place on evil, too, though I doubt they play by many rules.

With evil having been a prevalent part of our world's history through the written word and spoken languages, many speculations brew over the cause of such dark things. A person's or group of people's ability to speculate about evil is a part of our God given gift of having freewill. So I speculate, you speculate and who is to say truly who is right or wrong without the Word of God helping to direct our flow?

However and again, the freewill elements in this worldly society, helps to bring together other interesting perspectives. I've heard everything you can imagine coming to me in people's emails about what they believe to be the truth and origin about The Hat Man. I simply take it all in, hear it out, nod or do the horizontal head shake. Still and most importantly, I find it fascinating and am always hoping to learn more:

Dear Heidi,

I'm part of the Tuscarora Indian Nation of Western New York. The Tuscarora's were the 6th nation to join the Iroquois Confederacy. When I heard you speak of "The Hat Man" on your radio show—it gave me goose bumps! Especially when you said that some people describe him as looking like Abraham Lincoln.

For as long as I can recall, there have always been stories of what people on my Reservation call "The High Hat Man!"

Everyone who has ever seen him describes him as being very tall, dressed all in black and wearing a high hat. But no one reports ever having seen his face. Sightings of him go far back into our history. It's said that if you are under the influence of drugs or alcohol, then you shouldn't talk about him. It's also recommended that you not speak of him at nighttime, either.

I have heard stories from both Tuscarora and the Seneca people that this High Hat Man lives in swamps. There are some things said to help him stay away. This is why some Seneca's even put raw meat in the trees for him.

Within my family there have been two stories told to me about this High Hat Man. When my mom was younger, she was walking down the road to get to work one day. That's when she saw something in the corner of her eye. When she turned to look, it was the High Hat Man! He stood there only for a second glaring at her before he simply vanished.

Another time, my brother told me one of the scariest stories about him:

One night, my two cousins, my brother and dad were out driving around in the woods. My dad was in the passenger's seat and my cousins were in the back of the pickup truck my brother was driving. Sometime along their drive, my cousins noticed something moving behind them on the road.

They kept watching it until it came more within the direct path of the moonlight. That's when they really caught a glimpse of what it was—it was the High Hat Man! They both then started yelling at my brother to drive faster!

My brother couldn't hear exactly what they were saying. So he did the worst possible thing and stopped the truck to ask them, "What?" My cousins then became even more frantic as they yelled at him, "GO! GO!"

So my brother stepped on the gas to speed up as fast as he could. My cousins said that even though the truck was going faster, the High Hat Man just kept right up with them! The weird thing is, though the High Hat Man appeared to be walking at the same pace—he still kept up with them!

They said he was SO huge, that when he walked he would swing his long arms out towards them almost reaching them. Then all of a sudden he just faded away.

They were all creeped out for days after that!

It's no surprise to me that the knowledgeable Natives of North America, have an insight on the topic of The Hat Man. However, the roots of evil seems to have no definition to put our shovel into the ground to dig up the full dirt on them. But every little bit of information helps to paint the bigger picture of what we may be dealing with.

During my research, I came across a book by Jim Keith called *Casebook on the Men in Black*. It was in this book and among other resources, where a man in a dark suit has appeared during pivotal moments in our American history. A man in a dark suit has also appeared in association with occult and mystical practices. When it comes to Men in Black (MIB), they have more often been referred to as alien beings, or even humans who harass witnesses to UFOs.

Though when I think of a man in a black suit appearing during "occult and mystical practices" and appearing out of nowhere, I think of *only* The Hat Man doing such things. I believe outright, that The Hat Man and Men in Black are two different phenomena—although both have their similar "dark ties." Literally, they both might wear dark ties around their necks! ☺

All jokes aside, they really do come from the same Dark Source.

MIB's often appear in groups where they come in through a door to a person's home and speak out loud, even with witnesses around. MIB are quite physical in their appearance and physical in the way they go about doing things. They will knock on doors, drive cars, wear sunglasses, have varying degrees of skin tones/colors, speak with a robotic voice, or speak like a normal person would.

The Hat Man comes alone mostly, brings a feeling of pure evil and the name "devil" upon the lips of most who have seen him. He also likes to appear and disappear in an instant or through a real doorway, even if it leads to a closet or dead end. The Hat Man also could care less if you saw a UFO or astronaut—he's going to come to you regardless!

Both beings are bone chilling, but one is more soul chilling than the other.

Still, there are more differences between them to mention here that are truly important. The Hat Man comes to intrude upon the most innocent of us, the children—even mere toddlers. Not that toddlers have written to tell me, but people with really good memories of their toddler years have written to tell me of their first recollections of this horrific intruder:

Dear Heidi,

My encounter happened when I was less than two years old! It actually happens to be my very first memory from childhood, which is odd to hold on to from such an early age. I judge my age to be this young, because the occurrence happened while I was still in a crib and not able to climb the sides to get out!

So I'm really-really young, lying in my crib at my grandmother's house in a bedroom all by myself. That's when my memory begins with a shadowy Hat Man suddenly standing over me. I'm immediately and completely paralyzed, but I remember thinking about screaming!

Somehow, this shadowed figure communicated to me that if I were to make a sound—he would kill me! I don't know how—but I understood him completely!

This figure then reached down and put his hand on my chest. Then like a light goes off in my mind, that's all that I can remember! Oddly, since this encounter I have had a higher understanding of various things.

I now believe that this Hat Man is always in me or always near me in some form!

To threaten to kill a tiny-toddler of all people—really? It also makes you wonder at what level of communication that thing vibrates at to know how to push the thought of death towards a baby where it completely knows to comply to his commands! I wish I could banish the thought. But the horror continues:

Dear Heidi,

When I was a little kid, I had these reoccurring night terrors.

They would start where I'm in a dark alley and The Hat Man is running behind me, chasing me. He was a physical figure, but black with no discernible face. As he would get closer I would get more afraid where it felt like I was running through water until I couldn't move at all anymore. But somehow, I would always wake up right before he got to me.

In fact, I would often wake up to my dad holding me because I had been screaming bloody murder the whole time I was dreaming about this. I was also fully terrorized by these huge Shadow Spiders that would cover every surface of the hallway outside of my parent's bedroom. These things seemed to show up to prevent me from reaching my parents whenever I had these night terrors. This scenario of the nightmares and spiders happened over and over again for a few years.

When I was a toddler my parents even told me that what they thought was a "ghost," was constantly pushing me down the stairs! They said I would lurch forward as if someone shoved me, but no one could be seen actually doing this to me.

We moved before I got killed...

Dreaming of The Hat Man is actually nearly as common as people seeing him in person. His presence is one of certainty, where a witness to him knows he's something more profound than the imagination of a dream. In knowing that Shadow

Spiders are related to him and the dark actions of any phantom are, too, I feel comfortable in thinking that he took part in shoving this baby down the stairs. What would you do as a parent if you saw this time and time again happening to your toddler? I think these parents were wise to move.

Yet and still, his atrocities against the most innocent continue:

Dear Heidi,

It was my very first birthday when I first saw him—The Hat Man! The night prior to my birthday, my mum put me to bed at 11:30 PM. At midnight, my mum was in the living room when she heard something come across the new baby monitor. She said she heard me fighting and shouting over the monitor, but she thought it might be interference from another radio transmitting.

So, my mum went up to my bedroom where she was confronted by The Hat Man himself!

She said that I was physically fighting with him. The freaky part is my mum also said I was shouting at him with a deep voice. She said I sounded like a man might, though I was only one years old! Then the door to my bedroom quickly slammed shut in my mum's face so she couldn't get inside to help me!

This is the part that I remember:

The man was standing by the door as my mum began shouting and pounding on it to try and get inside. As he was standing there, he got the most hideous grin across his face. Then I started crying because he just scared me so much.

The man wore a top hat, long cloak with a sauté, a tie, a broach, and he had a sword in his left hand. I couldn't see his face clearly, since only a little light in the room showed a slight bit of his face.

Something strange happened when the door finally flew open on its own where my mum could finally come into the room. Though I don't know how—everything in my room was completely trashed! Even the bedroom door was hanging off from its hinges. Night after night, this Hat Man returned to terrorize me in the same manner. Mum finally got rid of my baby cot, so I just slept in her bed from then on.

Sometimes, my mum would pretend to be sleeping as we both heard him singing songs to me in a language that we didn't recognize. By my 6th birthday, he finally had gone...

No one is off limits when it comes to The Hat Man. This story sends shivers all over me, because here something so profoundly horrible was happening to this family and they had no one to turn to. It wasn't a possession, it wasn't a haunting and it wasn't something relatable to the common person. There was a man trashing a baby's room, slamming the door off its hinges and singing songs to a growing baby?! What the heck does one do in that situation?

But back to my point in showing the difference between MIB and The Hat Man:

Men In Black can be seen as comical in their awkward motions, often too stiff to even try to appear human. Oddly, these MIB were once a harassing force, fresh on the minds of those involved in UFO and alien topics. There was such a huge fear of being possibly approached by these guys, but now you don't hear so much about them.

In fact, when it comes to the thousands of emails and stories that I've been told over the years—I cannot recall ever getting anything close to being an MIB story. Believe it or not, I just came to that revelation just now while writing this! No one has told me anything that led me to believe, "Ah, you are wrong about that one—that's an MIB and not a Hat Man encounter."

So what does this tell me? (I'm thinking out loud now.) That tells me that things have changed out there!

I am pretty sure that if there were some MIB activity going on out there at a more regular rate (as it once was), I would have heard about it in some form. If I don't have my ear to the ground listening to what's abound in our world, someone sends me a random link to a story or I get an email seeking some honest advice from me about something paranormally inspired. Though I know that the whole MIB phenomena is not completely gone, (per my friend and fellow author on the weird, Nick Redfern) it is still greatly reduced from what I once perceived.

Digging into my spiritual sense and references to many science fiction movies—I cannot help but to wonder what the implications might mean in this major shift of dark lords. I admit that The Hat Man phenomenon has been happening to people for longer than before I named it. The MIB have also been stalking people for a number of years beyond my lifetime. But now, we hear of a more dominant presence and force, while another one hushes a bit?

That makes me want to create a little scenario to play out here:

Let's say that I'm a dark master lord who has a big pile of lowly minions dragging their knuckles on the ground for me when I command it. I tell them, "Drag thy knuckles and swing at anything that stands in the way of my commands. Make a clear path so that I can more easily walk along and prey upon my victims firsthand doing what I love to do best and feed upon them for myself!" Fresh meat is my fave!

So my knuckle-dragging minion's work tirelessly for years to clear the path I ordered so long ago, when suddenly, they are successful. Sure they had their little successes along the way where I got out and preyed upon a snack or two, but nothing like now!

I call back the knuckle draggers and tell them I can take it from here and so I do. Me, the dark lord master or master lord (or something like that), finally starts walking the Earth more freely. The obstacles were beaten down and the portals were opened more widely and so did the eyes of my victims.

Word starts to spread that I'm loose and visiting people. Finally! I'm getting the respect that I deserve and it's being dished my way in heaps. The fear in the world rises, and my feeding off from their fear rises along with my strength! Success is near, but I won't reveal my goal. Not yet…

That just got too real for me.

Something is changing in the world, rising and thundering up and into our souls while taking a piece of it. Why has this dark lord shown his face and name without fear of us preparing to deal with him? What does he know that we don't? Why is his presence alone enough for us to seek out God in the most urgent form in our lives?

Why is this happening and where is God in all of this?

I saw something once and I'm honestly hesitating to speak or write of it in here. It's something dear to me that I've not revealed to anyone before putting this down right now. In fact, I still don't feel it's the right thing to detail all of what I saw, because the message is what was most clear and important to share—which is this:

God has been weakened by our neglect.

I know that's a crazy-powerful statement to make, but I cannot help but to stand by it. God is all-powerful, omnipotent and is there for us in an instant when called upon. I didn't and won't ever say that God is dead or anything, because that's surely not the case. But to share more of what I mean:

Imagine having a child of yours never to return home, or say that they love you, or aim to make you proud—then you tell me if your heart gets ripped out of your chest or not! If you don't have kids, think of your parents or best friend who leaves you alone for an eternity without warning, never to show you love or concern—see if that depletes you at all. Think of it like a death of someone SO close to you that it hurts you to the core knowing you will never see their smile again.

Are you able to get to that painful place in your mind and heart now? Good.

Now multiply that feeling by a billion or so, of lost souls who were all connected to you because you created them!

Do you think this loss has weakened God even in the slightest? Do you think it hurts Him that even one of us He brought to life has turned their back on Him and went to the opposing side of His personal and universal war? You've become a Judas, a betrayer, a snitch, a rat, a lowlife, or dare I say—a knuckle dragging minion!

Don't think that God doesn't see what the darkness is doing to us. But the path got cleared for the darkness to come at us because we all lacked more than a little Faith in God. So, it can't be blamed on God as to why the darkness is here attacking us. But all is NOT lost because of its dark presence here, either.

I'm sure there are some people reading this who are shocked that I went the God route so directly and are wondering why this is in a paranormal book. Believing that the paranormal exists seems to be a new and exciting topic for a lot of people. But you should be grateful that you can express that interest so freely now; it's compliments from those of us who endured a whole load of crap (aka: ridicule) from the general public for years to get this far!

So, enjoy the emancipation of the paranormal believer and experiencer—because truly it was rough. But back to my point: Believing in the paranormal is now truly widely accepted—but when it comes to God bits (for some) a wall of questions comes up.

Ghosts and UFOs can be photographed to give some kind of evidence that they exist, so believing in them is often an easier feat with less doubt than thinking of God being around and present. But God is all in the planning of everything that exists today, so the evidence of The Creator is everywhere. From the perfect patterns of every diverse snowflake, to the strands of DNA that spells out all that we are. Something or someone had to decide how this world would be expressed the way that it is now.

I also am not going to give that credit to a tribe of aliens as having created this whole planet as some have—that's just not going to happen. The miraculous is all around us and miracles happen everyday to many of us. Here I am this fluffy paranormal researcher and even I felt I had to write about my encounters with Jesus who healed me of ailments that should have killed me over and over again!

Now, something compared to the likes of the devil is showing up and people are all chatting online about the existence of such a thing. There's astonishment and shock about it, but acceptance that The Hat Man exists. In a sense, his existence is even a bit easier to swallow and get the attention of others. Sure there are blogs and chats going on about angels and holy encounters with Jesus. But to be honest it's not what's hotly "trending"—if you know what I mean.

God stuff is ordinary, traditional and known in relation to Bible stories and television specials. The paranormal has pictures, videos and shocking reenactments that spur the imagination and gets us out hunting ghosts for ourselves to bring another reality near. I've yet to hear of "angel hunters" going out looking for this magnificent being that has appeared to someone who was in need. Now watch this be the next new trend on television since I mentioned it here. But that would be a show I'd watch with great enthusiasm and a great big bowl of popcorn (truth be told)!

This chapter was supposed to be about The Hat Man and his history, but look where it's led us—to something more important than focusing on his rotten trends. But yes, Hat Man and MIB's have been around for a long time wearing their similar suits for centuries, according to Jim Keith's book that I highly recommend to read. In fact, that book does such a good job in digging into the past on these dark suits, that I'm relieved to not have to do it. I really thought on rehashing the ins and outs of men in black suits appearing throughout time, but it's been done already. Besides, to dig into such a far reaching topic is well—not an easy feat and I can say it's not my expertise or purpose. My head isn't too big to admit my shortcomings, so I instead choose to focus in on what I have found, experienced and know that's going on today.

It's my hope that lifting the hat off of the head of this dark thief of innocence can be accomplished by arming people with knowledge of what's going on in the present and not the past. Getting and keeping your Faith in God to keep up in this all-out battle for your soul—this is the key. This is why I have done what *seems* like "jumping" from one topic to the next in my various books with my personal accounts and perspectives. Some don't understand the connections I'm making, but I think most have an inkling.

Speaking of soul battles:

Dear Heidi,

My frightening encounter with The Hat Man happened a few years ago while house sitting for a friend. My goal was to get their pasture watered before I left for the day. So, starting around 3:00 AM I set the alarm clock to wake me up every hour to go and move the water sprinkler around.

In between the alarm going off, I sort of dozed in and out of consciousness. At around 5 am or so, is when something strange happened. I felt my whole astral body essentially lift off from the bed and begin to move towards the door.

It was so frightening because I was aware I was moving, but I couldn't control the motion or move my body at all. I was floating, uncontrollably towards the bedroom door! That's when I saw a shadow standing in the hallway. It was a large, tall, and dark shadow of a man—with a hat. He was coming directly towards me and I was sure that he wasn't there for anything good.

Immediately, I started screaming and yelling for God! I even called out to good spirits and angels to just

help me! I was screaming at the top of my lungs as best and as much as I could!

I could feel and see my consciousness shift back and forth between my paralyzed-astral body and my struggling body still laying in my bed. I kept praying— then suddenly I woke up! I was back in bed and the shadow was gone.

I don't know what this whole incident meant and I have never seen him since. Just thought it was important that I share this with you...

If there were any doubt between the different tactics of the MIB versus The Hat Man, stories like this should help clear things up. If this were only a dream, why has it stayed with this person to know that something was different about this scenario. It's always astounding how people just know when they are in danger and what to take more seriously than other random thoughts and/or dreams.

It's also super awesome to hear when people know to call on their Faith in the face of The Hat Man. It kind of puts a big stall in his plans, even when his eyes are on the prize (i.e. your soul) and so close. Some people go about pushing their Faith forward and it always seems to hit the target where it hurts and stops The Hat Man:

Dear Heidi,

I was in a unique "dream state" when I saw myself sitting in a chair in my living room. I looked down my hallway and that's when I saw a shadowy figure with a hat (fedora style) and a black cloak.

He was *not* moving. But somehow I could clearly see the shadow that he cast on the floor, start to grow bigger and move towards me down the hall! As soon as

I saw him I felt the energy in my body get completely drained!

I started repeating over and over in my mind, "Greater is He that is within me than is in the world!"

I knew that if I did not manifest the feeling of the Holy Spirit—that I was going to die! That's how much this thing was draining me. Then my body started moving towards him—without any control. I rolled out of my chair, onto my hands and knees, while still trying to summon the will power to move my lips to speak in tongues.

Eventually, I was able to utter the first word. Then as I continued to utter more words, my energy began to return to my body. Then I spoke in tongues quicker and the attack ended immediately!

I have been attacked before in my dream states. Speaking in tongues always immediately ended the attacks, but the various attacks by The Hat Man were the first time that I was ever challenged in speaking in tongues.

This demon was different!

However people turn on the Faith, it doesn't seem to matter in the demise of The Hat Man. What a sneaky bastard (pardon my language) to go the route of tapping into pulling a person's soul out from their sleeping body?! Sometimes, though, it seems he might be successful in gaining the souls of those who go missing but were already forgotten:

Dear Heidi,

I'm what you might consider to be a psychic, though I don't officially put that out there as a profession or anything. I like to keep that part of my life to myself mostly, but lately, odd things have been going on. Two months ago I was driving up my street at night and I saw something odd standing under a street light. It was a shrouded being that looked like it was wearing a fedora hat.

I'm used to seeing the dead, but this felt like something different—something dark!

But I just shrugged off what I saw because I always see or hear weird things. Then a pattern emerged. I started seeing him again and again at different places, ever since that first day!

The scary part is, I've now noticed that spirits in graveyards are just...gone!

Normally when people die, it's been my experience that their spirit's stay attached to the body. So, I can't help but to wonder and feel that his sudden appearance is connected to their disappearance!

Now my friends are telling me that they've seen something like a black, misty man around town, too—wearing a hat! That made me realize that I'm not the only one who saw this thing watching and observing me. Now I know that he's done the same to my friends, as well!

To think that the battle continues on even into the next life?! Ugh, I shudder at the thought. When there's no escape from him even when you are 6 feet under, that's beyond the mirror of frightening. So now I'm even more certain that it's best that he's stopped before it ever even comes to that.

I believe it's best that we get our souls heading in the right direction right where we stand and breathe—right now! If The Hat Man is digging up disembodied souls, his numbers are growing tremendously. But how could he have such access to souls and is this really a true phenomenon indicated in this email sent to me? Could this be widespread or just centered in the area this person lived? I don't have access to a network of psychic's, but perhaps at some point more will reach out to me to lend their thoughts to this potential pattern.

Again I wonder how The Hat Man would have access to the souls of people who might linger near their graves. Then I remind myself on how he gains access to babies where he threatens their lives, so it seems he is crossing boundaries not limited by our assumed rules of what's sacred and protected. Whether we are ever able to fully define this Hat Man for what he is, that shouldn't matter. It's what he's already doing is what we should be most profoundly concerned about.

I've gone from writing on aliens, to Shadow People, to Jesus encounters, to an easier way to pray as taught by an angel, to now two (count them) TWO books fully on *Faith—The Other "F" Word*. Yes. That's part of the title of the books, too, "The Other 'F' Word." I did one for kids and adults, because Faith is THAT important in the face of all that is coming our way!

My mentioning these books (perhaps even repeatedly) may sound like an odd ploy to get you on to my next book, because it is and I don't care how it sounds when it comes to saving souls. I'm always as painfully honest as I can be when talking (or writing) on these topics, especially when it's on something I feel strongly about. Humor is my best friend, but always keeping things fluffy doesn't move the mountains needing to be shoved aside sometimes and damn—sometimes one has to shove!

Again—it's that important that we take a look at ourselves and get our Faith going in the right direction of having of no doubts, no reluctance, no weakness, no hesitance, no neglect and lots of patience until we get our Faith where it should be.

Prior to this book coming out, I had only ONE book involving Shadow People and aliens, both combined in that one book, *The Secret War*. I then had my *Picture Prayers* book out and *Jesus Is No Joke* book out, too. But guess which book I always got asked to talk about on radio and television? People wanted to know more ONLY about the spooky and dark stuff!

What does that tell you?

The priorities are goofed up out there, but we need to create and find a better balance for ourselves. Or else, we might trip over and fall unto the wrong side of the fence where no trespassing should be allowed. Be aware and be ready. It's my hope and warning that we all are ready, just so we might realize that we are worth a whole lot more than we think we are in the eyes of God, the dark one and the battle we *are* (without a doubt) in the middle of.

12

WHY DOES HE COME?:

Deserving?

People often ask me, "If this is the devil then why did he visit me?"

Somehow people feel as if they may have welcomed this rotten entity into their lives and wonder if they are indeed deserving of it in some form. I cannot say with certainty if they indeed did something to roll out the red carpet to darkness. However, I'm sure there are a multitude of methods to do that.

So, you might ask what could be done to trigger an invite to The Hat Man?

Well, let's look down the aisle to see what we have for sale on the shelves of mankind's, slip-ups, shake-downs, trips, dips and outright quips of endearment to the dark side. Well, you have your basics like the Ouija Board, which is known to open up a portal or two in ones home or mind. In fact I've had quite a few people write me saying that their troubles started by the laying of their hands upon the planchette of a Ouija Board.

So is playing a little "board game" really a devil's calling?

Not necessarily, but you sure weren't looking for butterflies and angels when you started upon the board—were you?

Nope! You were looking to be scared, talk to the dead, and you were more than likely looking at the "other side" that might have a touch of darkness in its corner. Your mind was opened to the possibilities and you literally stuck your fingers into the eyes of what's able to look back at you.

Now what did I say about the Ouija Board not necessarily being an invitation to the darker side? Okay, so I could be wrong. Because this does look a bit like an opportunity for something to look into that newly opened mind of yours.

Dear Heidi,

I personally have never seen this Hat Man guy. But a few years ago, he followed my friend around for a few months—where he would just showed up at random!

The story my friend told me began with him and a few friends playing with a Ouija board in one of their basements. One of them was doing all of the talking who just so happened to speak in Latin at the board, I might add. The rest of them kept their eyes and mouths shut.

My friend, Mike, heard someone say his name and against his friend's advice he answered the voice. Immediately, the candles went out! The guy who was doing all of the talking got upset, because he was afraid that they let something out. So they all quickly went back upstairs while scolding my friend.

Once upstairs, the doorbell rang. One of the other friends went and answered the door. No one else could see the door from where they were. The friend just stood silently at the door for a few seconds before saying the door was for my friend, Mike.

It was The Hat Man!

He stood there with glowing red eyes for almost a minute before disappearing. He then started to

reappear at random for a few months, sometimes visible to others, sometimes not. The fact that the guy who answered the door knew who The Hat Man wanted makes me wonder if he can talk or communicate via some other means.

Anyways, two years later while ghost hunting, my friend and his two friends saw The Hat Man again. They were on the grounds of a closed mental hospital . That's when The Hat Man showed up and literally chased them from the cemetery where they were standing at the mental hospital!

I don't think Mike has seen it since then. The cemetery incident was just over a year ago. But it followed them all the way back to their car as they ran.

In addition, another friend of mine described seeing something similar to The Hat Man, but he held an actual conversation with it. The Hat Man outright claimed to be the devil. When my friend told it to leave, he had a streak of really bad luck after that!

Anyways, I hope you find this helpful. I kind of want to see the man for myself. But I'm kind of reluctant...

All from a Ouija Board and answering a disembodied call?!

There are of course tons of ways that darkness can be invited in, another being the use of magic or the practice of looking into deities other than the One True God. I'm talking about looking into the outright worship of mother nature (I refuse to capitalize the name as some do). What else can I be speaking of except for white magic, black magic and the Wiccan beliefs. Yes, I have met many Wiccan's who have claimed to have a balance in their beliefs in worshipping the elements of nature and have their Faith in God, too.

But there's lots of wiggle room in there for something sinister to slip in while you are focusing on your particular deity of the moment with a dash of God in there. It's equivalent to looking at traffic lights ONLY for the Green Light—because everything goes! If you didn't acknowledge the Red Light ever on what not to do, then you are bound to have LOTS of collisions ahead in your spiritual life.

I don't know where my analogies come from to be honest. ☺

Limits are needed in some instances and they aren't always there to just restrict a person's mind or growth, but to help protect against unnecessary head-butts with evil. So for those who think if you do a dab of things on the darker side, like casting a spell over someone to do what you'd like and then you say your prayers every night—this isn't a good balance! There is some common sense needed for all things in life.

I personally know a good number of people who claim to be Wiccan and they aren't negative people who aim to do harm so they shouldn't be hunted or anything. But to seek out power through the elements of nature that we all know exists to a certain extent, it just feels like the human ego driving people once again. This is my opinion and we all have them, but continually distracting away from God to focus on a creation of His is unnecessary when you can just go to Him and stand behind Him.

Think of it like this:

Mankind made shoes, but what if a group of people decided to worship the power of shoes. They protect our feet, guide us down roads and allow us to climb mountains and dive to the deepest depths of oceans. Oh–the power of the shoe! Ceremonies are held to walk over hot coals with fire retardant shoes on, while good food is grilled and people sit around conversing with others sharing on how blessed they are to have shoes on their feet. So much time is wasted on the worshipping of shoes that the bigger picture gets missed that most have access to shoes, but it's not as big of a deal as it's made out to be. Because it's already known that there's strength in having a good pair of shoes, but most people are using them to get to where they need to be in life so they can reach out to The One who made it all possible—God! Stopping on the road to worship the shoes that are helping you walk down the road towards God, well, it just honestly makes no sense.

Okay, off the topic of shoes and Wiccan's now and into The Hat Man's irritating presence...

Then there are the more common instances that I hear the absolute most about when it comes to The Hat Man showing up—that's when it comes to the abuse of drugs and alcohol. These sorts of instances are the ONLY times that people feel somehow responsible for The Hat Man tipping his hat in their direction. It doesn't matter if the person tells me at the beginning, middle or end of their Hat Man encounter that they reveal their dependency on something—they somehow know it's related to him showing up. I'm not talking about the person who has some fun every once in awhile who goes out to get tipsy with some drinks and friends. So don't worry that you are going to Hell in a hand-basket for your night on the town just yet. Then of course a "little" drug abuse is never okay to do and think you can get away from the risks involved with that physically, mentally or spiritually.

Dear Heidi,

My life has been going through drastic changes after the event I'm about to share with you. One night, I was high on meth and I was getting super paranoid, so I went outside for some fresh air. When I looked up, there was a dry lightning storm that looked very condensed. As the sky lit up—I saw *him*. With each lightning spark, I felt his presence grow!

My instant thought was, "Oh shit! They're here!"

He was standing on the deck of the next-door neighbor's house—just staring at me! I could also see various other Shadow People off in the distance. This is when my life began to go absolutely crazy for three years—but I don't feel like typing that all out right now (because my typing sucks)!

On a good note: I'm happy to say that I'm sober now and have found Jesus!

Then there's:

Dear Heidi,

I've had two experiences in the past month or so with this Hat Man. Lately, I have been interested in the paranormal and on a self-proclaimed spiritual quest. I've actually had some great success in doing astral projection on numerous occasions.

The first time I saw this man I didn't know what it was.

It happened during a projection when I saw him standing on the corner of a nearby street. The second time, I saw him in my bedroom—just a few days ago! I watched as he walked into my bedroom. Then he slowly and methodically walked towards the bed and jumped onto my bed and started attacking me and my wife!

However, I wasn't scared! I was more like, "WTF is happening here?!"

Then I told one of my friends about it and described what this guy looked like with a wide hat and trench coat. A few days later my sister told me that her friend thinks it was the "demon of my addictions"—which I believe it was!

How so very interesting and disappointing that people know of the draw of The Hat Man and yet were still stuck with him due to their past or even current dependency. It was even more intriguing when I heard from those who recovered from being dependent on drugs or alcohol, also removed The Hat Man from their lives! So does that mean the drugs or brews were cursed by The Hat Man himself or any of his minions? Of course not!

When anyone tips back a few too many drinks, doesn't that make you a bit less inhibited? Might you perhaps say and do things that you wouldn't do otherwise without the power of the cocktail behind you backing you up? Some might call it "liquid courage," while I call it the "moral inhibitor." The Hat Man might call it, "an opportunity to your lifeline!"

When you are under the influence of alcohol, your guard is down and you are more at ease. For one like The Hat Man who likes to prey upon the less guarded soul—you might be what's for dinner! All it takes is for one scrape to get an infection that can take a limb or a life. You might think, "If only I hadn't stumbled and fallen and scraped my knee or at least gotten my Tetanus shot in-time, then maybe I would have been okay." You can also think, "If only that Tetanus bacteria wasn't living on the surface I scraped my knee on, I'd have been okay." But the fall happened causing the scrape and the

Tetanus was just doing what it does—existing and infecting when the opportunity came. The Hat Man does no less than wait for your wound or weakness to become apparent and he leaps at the opportunity!

It should be quite a scary notion to know that, actually.

So many people don't want to tease a Great White Shark by going out into the open ocean if they have a bleeding wound, but just imagine doing that for a minute. You are all alone, floating out on the ocean and you've just so happened to cut yourself on a rock. You have no way to know when a shark will catch the scent of blood in the open ocean, but you know with every fiber of your being that one eventually will spot you out!

Now imagine you are a solo soul with a weeping soul wound thanks to the end of a wine bottle, pill or needle. You stumble through the streets with a group of friends and your soul scent is dripping down to whatever disgusting hole The Hat Man comes from. Just as with the shark, you don't know when but at some point he will come if you continue to leak your scent of exposed-soul weakness. This is not just a scenario I'm painting here, this is the reality going on everyday!

This Hat Man is a predator and the chances that he will look each of our ways are nearly guaranteed at some point. How close he actually gets is up to us as individuals and I will go more into that a little later in this book. But the message is to be aware of the predator, so you can at least be on-guard to some extent.

Still, for anyone to think that they "deserve" the likes of the devil to come after them—that's a bit of a stretch. I feel as if some of the people who write me with that dangling question are truly asking me if I think they are essentially "screwed" in matters of their soul. But I retract and instead say that there is only one Judge who answers that question and that is God, of course.

However, it's important to know that some people can answer that question for themselves until that day comes that they are truly Judged. We do know ourselves best and if there are things we need to work on from the inside-out. So if you know there's work to be done—then do the work! Get yourself feeling right about yourself, life and soul.

Truth be told, we all are in this life together—but we die and are Judged alone. So moving along with the "traffic" won't matter when you get pulled over by a critical police officer. The officer caught you and it will be you alone who are asked why you were speeding when you knew the speed limit!

But before you think "spiritually screwed" is your new nickname just because The Hat Man has waved to you or tipped his hat—know that some people's only apparent mistake is that they were born! As I've mentioned, The Hat Man LOVES to terrorize children! Just when you think there are rules to his game, all of that is thrown out of the window when he pokes his wretched head into a child's bedroom!

Dear Heidi,
I have had several encounters with what you call "The Hat Man." When I was about three years old, I was sleeping with my parents in my grandparent's basement. I was laying on a pad or a low mattress where we all slept in the back of the laundry room. There was no door, only a sheer bathroom shower curtain for a little privacy.

Standing right behind this curtain, was a man approximately 7-feet tall with a hat on and what looked like a long coat! My parents would try to explain to me that it was only the bathroom or clothes hanging at an odd angle casting this shadow. I saw him every night that I looked towards the doorway. Eventually, I told myself he was the Bogeyman! I thought, "If I'm good today then he won't be there." So, on the days I felt I was good he wasn't there so I didn't bother even looking for him.

Other days I would just hope he wasn't there.

Later on when I was 8 years old, I saw what I now know to be The Hat Man! As I was playing with my dolls, I watched him walk out of my mother's doorway and directly into the wall. I was super scared, I didn't know what a ghost was and didn't have a name for this Bogeyman from my past.

I later found out about The Hat Man when I decided to read some ghost stories online. As I scrolled through some, I saw something about "Shadow People." This led me to something called "The Hat Man." I froze for a minute as I read the descriptions of the same guy who I called my "Bogeyman." I finally felt validated as I went to tell and show my mom about this guy.

Oddly enough, not only did my mom believe me, but she went on to tell me about her own personal sighting of him! She said she was sitting on her bed talking to a friend about a boyfriend she just broke up with because of his physical abuse and drug dealing. During the conversation, in the doorway there suddenly appeared this tall-hatted figure! Just as quickly as he appeared, the bed they were sitting on started to shake violently!

When my mom told me this, that's when we realized we had both experienced the same thing. Now I'm trying to face my fears about this whole thing and want to learn more about his intent. Any info you can share on this topic would be greatly appreciated and thanks.

What could a child as young as three have done to deserve The Hat Man showing up to terrorize them? In this lifetime, that answer is: There isn't *anything* done deserving of him to visit *anyone*. NONE of us are deserving of him!

An interesting pattern noted here in this story and among many, is the family bloodline. It seems that The Hat Man pays attention to bloodlines and lineage. This isn't always the pattern of going from mom to child, sometimes it's an uncle or grandfather who has experienced him. Then there are, of course, no patterns in his methods often times. Yet, many are able to relate the timing of when The Hat Man shows up.

Dear Heidi,

My boyfriend and I both have had experiences with The Hat Man. Only, The Hat Man we saw was a little different. Basically, he was a "Wyatt Earp" type of Shadow. The brim of the hat wasn't as wide as others— think more like a literal Shadow Cowboy!

My boyfriend used to see him in his house as a kid, including different places throughout his adult life. He would wake up in the middle of the night and they would look directly at each other. Then this "person" would tip his hat to my boyfriend, turn, walk and fade away!

There was one incident that turned violent with this Hat Man. My boyfriend was 18 at the time and had just moved into an apartment complex with a roommate. One night he woke up out of some instinct and the room was darker than normal, but the television was on. He said he saw the Cowboy Hat Man, but he still doesn't think it was the same one he usually saw.

Then he said it slowly put pressure on his chest to the point to where he couldn't breathe—at all! As he started to grow limp The Hat Man grabbed him and started

jerking him up and down on the couch! He remembers looking at the television and could tell he was bouncing up and down.

My boyfriend then said the name of "Jesus"—and it fled!

A few minutes later he heard a woman scream about 50 yards from his back porch, so he went outside to look around, but never saw anything. A few hours later, he found out from other people in the community that a prostitute had been murdered a little over 50 yards away from his apartment. He said that was the only scary encounter he has had with this Shadow Figure. The other times, he said he wasn't and hasn't been scared at all of him.

The experience I had was a little different. My father was dying. You know how you can see a reflection of whatever is around in someone's eyes if you look closely enough? Well, my dad had suffered a traumatic brain injury that led him to have a major stroke. He lost the ability to move one of his eyes and was given about another hour to live. This was after a three-week battle of doctors trying to save him.

Well, I sat down in front of him and noticed instantly that the eye he had lost control of, he could move it up the wall. Then with his other eye he would look at the ceiling—he was looking at something! When he would bring his eyes to the ceiling, they would get really wide— like he was absolutely terrified!

He couldn't control his eyes for very long, so they would fall back to the side. He just kept doing this, gasping for air every time he looked up at the ceiling. It was so obvious something was scaring him, that I leaned forward and saw a reflection in his eyes. What I saw in his eyes terrified me—it was The Hat Man!

Again, this thing was more of a Wyatt Earp with a smaller brimmed hat, arms crossed and head leaned up against wherever he was standing. I didn't feel scared, not for anyone in that room. I just felt scared for my dad, because he seemed so frightened.

I know it could've just been his brain/head trauma, but I knew he was seeing something. He could've just been scared because his body was giving up when he was only 42 years old. I don't know. I know what I saw, though.

Since then, my family and I pray.

We do still have weird occurrences, I sometimes even dream of things before they happen. I've been dreaming a lot recently about the end of the world. Not as though the world is going to explode or implode—but almost like a huge war will take place.

Wherever we have moved to, there are always strange occurrences. Lights constantly flickering, TV turning off and on, and our baby talking and cooing to things we can't see. My nine-year-old daughter climbs into bed with me constantly saying there is a man who lives in her closet and this man scares her. I also get an extremely high-pitched ringing in my ears within 24 hours prior to something happening that's odd.

I don't know what all of this means, but as I sit here and type this, my dining room light keeps turning off and on.

I've prayed, and asked others to pray for me. I have to ask though...honestly wondering...I don't feel like I am doing what I am supposed to be doing in my life. I have this impending feeling that I am supposed to be here, in the city in which I live, but that I am supposed to be doing something else. I'm just kind of lost, my family and I are trying to figure out what's going on.

Have you ever heard of anything like this?

It's not rare or strange for a person who has experienced The Hat Man to have other strange phenomenon going on around them. This sort of pattern emerges with people who have had alien encounters or even just a basic haunting. Electrical phenomena, high pitched ringing in the ears and psychic phenomenon all happen with alien abductees—and as you can read with The Hat Man victims, too.

Why is this? It's because it's all connected.

Now, if we want to go far out in our thinking here, we can surmise another reason why some kids have experienced The Hat Man while others have not (minus the family connection). There is the very real possibility that the child is a true bright light that The Hat Man wants to stomp out before the child reaches their full potential. There seems to be a very real pattern here that people who say they have seen this Hat Man since they were a child, feel that they have different abilities than the next person:

This is the continued thought of the previously detailed story of the child that was under the age of two, who couldn't crawl out from their crib yet:

I must say that I possess some uncontrollable psychic abilities, as does my mother, one of my younger sisters, and my grandmother! My grandmother says its in our blood, passed down? Additionally when I have had my palm read, the reaction I observe from the reader is that of pure confusion stating that I have unique lines. I could literally sit here for days describing my almost constant day-to-day psychic happenings, but that's not what I'm writing you about.

Here's the continued perspective of the story mentioned of the child who kept being pushed down the stairs:

When you said that their goal could be to blot out your light (on the radio show) that struck a cord with me, Heidi. I have a very strong intuition about people and certain things that has had me drawn to the mystical and supernatural since I was a kid.

It does seem like maybe they were trying to stop me from realizing my potential by getting to me while I was young. There are many other instances of strange occurrences and attacks of a supernatural nature in my life, besides the Shadow People and The Hat Man.

It would seem that perhaps those who are impressed upon by this Hat Man, could serve as the eyes and ears for those of us who cannot see evil so readily. They may even be beacons of light who can protect the rest of us by simply being able to warn us when something is near like The Hat Man and what his intensions might be at the moment. So, gaining access to them while they are young to steer them one way over another, could be an angle of The Hat Man. Perhaps simply by scaring the specially sighted child to not want to "see" or use their special gifts in any form, might be what's inspired by seeing The Hat Man. Some might even turn to numbing their insight via drugs or alcohol, or they get overwhelmed to the point of inspiring mental illness to settle in.

Dear Heidi,

At about 7 years old I awoke in the middle of the night to see a Christ-like figure (I am leery to say it was Him) sitting in my rocking chair in my bedroom. I asked if it was time. He said no, he was just watching over me—that I was to do many great things.

Later at the age of 14, I lost my innocence. This is when I gave up on life and seriously considered suicide. I had come to the conclusion that I would never have a girlfriend and that I could never have any meaningful type of social life. It was at this point in my life that things really started to get interesting.

I had always felt like something was watching me and in time those feelings grew stronger.

One night I went to bed and as I started to drift off to sleep I came upon a thrashed looking wheat field. The smell of the wheat was extremely strong in the air. I was actually lying in the field when I started to sit up, but as I struggled to, I felt an enormous weight upon my chest.

Then appeared the Horsemen!

Seven hooded figures appeared out of nowhere and rode in a circle around me. Their arms stretched to cover my mouth as they rode around me. As they did this, instantly, I could not breathe and this continued for what seemed like an eternity. I finally awoke and found myself upright in my bed covered with sweat and my shirt and sheets scattered about my room!

I had physical visitors almost nightly through my teen years.

They ranged from one of the hooded Horsemen to what I would describe as "watchers." The watchers were generally very benign. Typically they would show up and quietly watch to see what I was doing. Occasionally they would be brave and almost ask questions. Typically I got the, "Who are you?" Other times I got, "What are you doing?" Sometimes I heard, "What are you?" Almost as if I were something other than human. The really bold ones would tell me that I was different, that I glowed.

Once I left home things grew quiet for about a month. I set up my apartment and my grandmother warned me to never use the closet in my bedroom. I thought nothing of it and went on about life. About a month after moving in, it started—boy did it ever!

Again it was a dark hooded figure. The temperature in the apartment would drop 10 to 15 degrees instantly. Light bulbs would pop as I walked through the house. Once, I changed 12 bulbs in one night. The TV would come on, change channels, volume up and down. The VCR would rewind halfway through a movie. Worst of all at night when I slept, or tried to—it came out! I can only describe him as the "dark man."

He was always dressed in a cape and a top hat. Often times he would just hover over me. On the rare occasion, he would shake my bed violently until I awoke completely frozen with fear!

I met a friend and she seemed to be understanding of what I was going through. I took her to my home and watched her reaction as the phone rang, though no one was there. We were amazed as the air conditioner was running full blast yet the temp rose 15 degrees instantly.

I have a 4 year old now and want only to protect her. Occasionally, I check what is going on around me in a spiritual sense. About every 6 months I go through a cleansing ritual marking the doors and windows of the house with Jordan River water. I have managed to protect my home and remain safe there for several years now. My visitors have rarely returned and until recently the dark man never came.

Then it happened. He showed up at my door—laughing at my feeble attempts to protect my family. I once again resorted to what I knew best. I focused my spiritual energy and blasted him. As always before—he went away.

He is gone for now and I am thankful. I only hope that I can better prepare myself for his next visit.

Truly a devastatingly, horror-filled story, to say the least. Was it easily overlooked or noticeable how much more comfortable this person was in mentioning seeing and experiencing this Hat Man—but NOT Jesus? They state that they are "leery to say that it was Him." Why is it more believable that evil paid a visit rather than holiness?

It seems that this Hat Man has indeed been successful, even in this case. Here already we can see how some of our gifted ones might begin to doubt themselves and their perceptions to what's most important for all of us—to know that God is watchful and accessible when darkness is near. In their dream, the hooded Horsemen stretched out their hands to cover their mouth—and it worked to an extent.

The moment this person felt weak and wanted to die, a message was somehow sent to the one who would more than love to have access to their soul. This Hat Man and his lingering presence of dread, horror and negativity, even invited other related darkness into their life and dreams. It's as if a target gets painted on the ones who can bear witness to other existences if they dare show human weaknesses, or not. Like it kicks open the door to dark possibilities that the victim doesn't always know how to close. This person luckily was able to, sort of.

This Hat Man is a sly character and he's been doing this taunting for a *very* long time. He comes, then he leaves, only to return successfully to make a point. That then must mean that something he's doing works at times. Obviously, that's not always the case.

Then there is the other real possibility that an agreement was made to work for The Hat Man in this lifetime—even by those who appear to be innocent.

I know, who would agree to such a thing—right?

When it comes to the Light side of things, I can say with certainty that agreements are made to work for good. How do I know this? It's because I made such an agreement myself! I already know the thoughts flowing out there about the impossibility of such a thing, because I wouldn't have thought that to be ever possible myself. Yet, it's true.

It's a story I've put out there WAY too many times already in my other books and on the airwaves (concerning seeing what I knew to be called The Source and essentially agreeing to be born), so to get into the finer details again isn't so much needed. What took place, brought me full-circle in understanding my role here during this lifetime to help move things along in a direction for others to understand what is REALLY important. Which is: To help inform people of the threats to our souls, igniting Faith in the hearts of others, and inspiring how to defend ourselves—all while just being painfully honest and flawed in sharing as best as I can.

Now then, getting back to the notion of these unholy encounters with The Hat Man being done to those who "deserve it." After writing my book, "*Jesus Is No Joke*" based on my own holy encounters with Jesus—I can tell you that I didn't feel I deserved to see Jesus. In fact, I haven't heard of anyone tout that they think they are deserving to have Jesus appear to them personally!

I've had miraculous healings thanks to Jesus appearing and still I don't think I was exactly worthy of His Presence. Then again, I don't see why any of us doubts that He will appear to each of us one day. Because one thing that I know after my encounters with Jesus, is that He is MORE than aware of each of us and every issue! Sadly though, darkness is aware, too.

Case and point:

More recently (June of 2013), as is usual, my coworker friends like to find out more about my world inside of the paranormal at random times. Two particular coworkers I will call Jasmine and Cheryl, just so happened to have never heard me chat on the topic very much before. So of course, if someone asks me about it I oblige. So I grazed the surface of everything from aliens to angels to Shadow People. For some reason on this particular day, I really dug into the topic of The Hat Man. This topic always gets people's attention that the devil incarnate can be so busy in already showing up as he does.

We must have chatted for a good 30 minutes as we all tied up our paperwork. Cheryl had to go home, while myself and Jasmine still had more to do. I remained in the office doing my final billing for the day for my patients, while Jasmine still had to gather one more patient to be seen. Jasmine brought the patient down to the therapy gym and led him to go in-between the parallel bars to assist him in standing. I heard a bit of chattering coming out from the gym, only to have Jasmine suddenly come running into the office urging me to come out to hear what her patient was exclaiming.

So I went out to the patient and he was pointing at the mirror that covered the full-length of the entire wall, which helps patients right their posture for standing and walking. As I got closer to the patient, he was saying, "Who is this guy who doesn't speak English? I can't understand him!"

Jasmine started in to say, "He was saying there's a man in black standing here, but I don't see anyone. Heidi, it sounds like The Hat Man you were *just* talking about!"

Neither Jasmine nor I could see anyone in the room but the three of us. The patient continued to point at the mirror and exclaim how the man in black was standing right there. Jasmine told him that he was just pointing at himself. The patient was stern to say, "I'm not pointing at myself! He's moving around—now he's behind you! Now he's over there!"

Jasmine and I got the chills as we watched the patient take his stare away from the mirror and look stunned when he saw no one was physically standing behind us.

As soon as he returned his glance back to the mirror, he seemed to realize that he was looking at something not quite normal as he continued to say that he was still there. I wanted to be sure of what he was witnessing, so I dared to ask, "Is he wearing a hat?"

The patient looked at me angrily and said, "Of course he has a hat on! You can see him right there!"

Just then-the patient was done with the conversation, though we did our best to assure him we just wanted to hear more details. This elderly patient, though he was forgetful, was quite aware and very stubborn. To put it simply, he was a Boston Irishman, so once his mind was made-up—that was it!

"Get me out of here then! You gals are acting like I'm crazy and you don't see him standing right there?! I'm done! Take me back to my room!" At the top of his lungs he yelled this as he pushed his wheelchair with full-force to back out from between the parallel bars. Jasmine obliged and wheeled him to the elevator to return him to his room.

Interestingly enough, on his ride in the elevator he quickly calmed down as he waved Jasmine to lean in closely as he said, "Look into my eyes. You can see that I'm not crazy— don't ya?"

When Jasmine returned, she and I were completely stunned.

Jasmine was more stunned with terror and wouldn't let me leave prior to her leaving, though I was already done with my patient's paperwork. I was more stunned to see how close The Hat Man had been listening in on my conversations about him.

"He was that close and near that he heard us?!" I thought over and over.

For me, the message was loud and clear—that he had me on his radar! I already had that inclination that he knew I was working against him by warning others of his threat. Yet, I had no such direct response before by him to show up right next to me to someone-merely 20 minutes after giving my warning about his existence!

I always say, that I take it nearly as a compliment when the dark side acts up in my direction. To me that means that I must be doing something right that they got so riled up! Well this time it was just too close and too near and it gave me a very unsettling feeling.

Jasmine, well, she didn't need any convincing about the reality of his presence—she had seen enough already!

The next day, Jasmine and I told all of the other therapists about what happened right after we had our discussion about The Hat Man. Everyone was fascinated and seemed to find it more than intriguing by our wide-eyed chatter about this spooky event. Then Cheryl, who had joined in on our initial chat about my paranormal work the previous night, said something I wish she hadn't. "Awe, I wish I was here to see that happen!" She stated.

I was quick to tell her to be careful what she wished for.

I then had to gather a patient of mine, so I was just about to head up onto the floor to go to my patient's room for a bit.

Unbeknownst to me, Jasmine needed to gather that same patient again who saw The Hat Man the evening before. I saw him get wheeled into the gym before I went upstairs, so I asked him if he remembered what happened the day before. He didn't have a clue on what I was talking about. Like I said, he was forgetful, but he didn't hallucinate and was otherwise quite aware.

I then headed to my patient's room and returned about 10 minutes later. When I finally returned with my patient to the therapy gym, everyone was chattering my way about what took place.

"Heidi! He came again!" I heard someone exclaim.

The same patient was placed inside of the parallel bars and as Jasmine walked away for a moment to prepare to stand him, the patient leaned towards the mirror. Another therapist reported seeing the patient talking at the mirror and saying things like, "No, I don't want no part of this. What's that? No!"

Then the therapist asked him who he was talking to and he said the man in black standing here. Then as if something got said to the patient by the man in black, the patient suddenly became near panicky. "Get me out of here! I don't want nothing to do with him! That man is no good! He's no good, I tell ya!"

Jasmine once again pulled him out from the bars to calm him down. The gym was full of activity and people at that time, so the patient seemed to be more at ease to stay in the gym and still complete his therapy. Another therapist even reported him saying to her, "Look at me! Do I look crazy to you?! That guy is no good over there!"

After being told about all of this, I also approached the patient and asked what the guy looked like and he was short to say, "Black suit, black hat and he ain't no good!"

It's said that God can be anywhere and everywhere at once. Jesus has shown up at various times in a blink of an eye when many ask for His help. It doesn't seem as if God or Jesus is broken into little pieces when He comes, either. When people like myself have been met with Jesus, you feel the whole of Him in your presence, giving you His full attention. There is only one Jesus and one God who are part of the same source of goodness able to do so much at once.

When it comes to The Hat Man, some people believe there's more than one out there.

I admit that there are differences in the reports of him being clean shaven, having a goatee of a beard, or wear various hat types, and so on. However, how do we know for certain if there's more than one? This Hat Man comes from a dark source all of his own and if he is indeed the devil—I don't see why he couldn't be in more than one place at a time. I've only had a report or two from people claiming to have seen more than one Hat Man at a time. So I lean more towards there being one central entity we are all dealing with. Just as we reach out to the One God-this rotten thing can reach out to all of us.

Even when in the midst of various Shadow People, the single Hat Man entity seems to be a central figure:

Dear Heidi,

I have been dealing with this phenomenon for as long as I can remember, so I have more stories than I can possibly relate in just one sitting. The one which I most wanted to relate to you was this one:

When I was 19, I was staying the night with my boyfriend. On this particular evening, I had been seeing Shadow People all night. They seemed to be following us all the while we walked around the small town in

which we lived. When we returned to his house later that evening, I lit several candles to say my usual evening prayers before we went to bed for the night.

My boyfriend had a strange feeling suddenly come over him and felt drawn to look out of the bedroom window. As soon as he did I heard him start to swear, so I went to see what was going on. Looking down out of the window, I could see dozens, if not hundreds of Shadow People surrounding the house!

As we backed away from the window and turned around, we saw there were about a dozen Shadow People in the room with us! But there was also a "Hat Man" standing in the middle of them!

My boyfriend was panicked, but having dealt with them for as long as I have, I knew to remain as calm as I could. I then took a deep breath and envisioned all of my love gathering into a "ball" in my hands, infusing it with the Light of God, as well. When I released my breath, I sent the "ball" straight at the "Hat Man" who was now approaching us with the other Shadow People behind him.

The effect of this "ball of love and light" can only be described as a flare in the darkness. My boyfriend actually shielded his eyes with his arm from the bright light that suddenly "flared!

They left.

What a horrifying ordeal! This is one even I don't know if I'd been able to stay conscious until the end of it! With this story alone, it can be easily speculated that The Hat Man reigns over the Shadow People and that he is not equal to them— but far superior! It's as if the Shadow People are his minions wreaking havoc and following the orders they are given.

Looking at the phenomenon of The Hat Man making his presence known in the lives of many for years, yet again. I don't think anyone should feel they deserve to have him taunting them, either. Even for me, more recently, he has tried to show himself to me:

After The Hat Man appeared to the patient at work, I had a feeling his eyes were indeed aiming to get another look at me. Prior to this event I'm about to detail, I had not seen him or felt him personally. Part of that still remains to be true.

Over the years of being bombarded with Shadow People and other negative entities, I became extremely strong on the spiritual front in protecting myself and my home from intruders. I'm not certain if The Hat Man saw that I was steadily working on this book here, or he saw that I got his message on being near when he showed up after hearing me talk about him. Whatever triggered this event—it was triggered:

I awoke one night because I felt the presence of something extremely dark, unmistakably dark, glare my way! This presence stood in front of the double, French doors that were already wide open, leading into my bedroom. With my eyes purposely remaining closed, I felt this presence step inside the room.

I told "it" and myself that I wouldn't give it the pleasure of seeing fear in my eyes. As this presence continued to stand still near the foot of my bed, I knew it was waiting for me to acknowledge it. Being smug in wanting more out of me, I felt it think up a different approach. It then slowly and methodically laid across the foot of my bed! Then, I felt it prop itself up on one elbow as if preparing to wait for as long as it would take, until I satisfied it by looking its way.

I felt myself oddly wait to see what it was wanting or would do, as I laid quietly with my eyes gently shut, but my mind wide awake. I then got a real sense of a pressed suit and the stiffly ironed seams of pant legs strewn across the bottom of my bed as the weight of a "man" became evident.

"It's him!" I felt nearly certain.

I decided that I wasn't going to let him get anymore comfortable than he already was. So I went to Who I knew best would sweep up the dirt of darkness. I then went to utter His Name and this is when I found that my mouth wasn't willing to work as I was normally used to. I felt as though forming words were new to me, while I oddly contorted my jaw to speak. Imagine having a mouth full of peanut butter and having your mouth numbed by a dentist, all at the same time!

I struggled to speak, and I swear I felt as if this thing smiled in delight as he antagonized me like a child who might say, "You can't get me now!"

"J-Jesus!" I finally got it out.

"Poof!" He was gone.

I didn't have to "get him," because Jesus was also within earshot just waiting to be tagged in to take care of the bothersome creep!

I knew that he knew of me, there were too many close calls for him not to. But never had he looked directly my way before. I took this encounter as an odd introduction of sorts. It was like he wanted to get a respectful load of fear from me and was willing to wait around for all of the accolades. His arrogance irritated me, more than anything. It also made me wonder where he found a way in at me.

Flash forward, April of 2014 and I'm nearly done with this book you are reading.

I'm lying in bed when I get an almost familiar sense come over me. As mentioned, I'm someone who can have very lucid dreams or even astral travels where I leave my body and go off adventuring. But before something like this happens, I almost get a twinge in my soul that wakes me up to what's about to happen. I then have the choice to sort of wake up into it to "steer" where I want to go, if I want to go and what I'm open to seeing or experiencing. It used to happen more than it does now, but I wonder if it just continues to occur and I just don't always recall it happening.

So to continue; I get this sense that I'm about to go on an adventure of the spiritual sort and I'm excited. Then I feel an external tug at the inner me to go "somewhere." I was like, "Oh here we go, Heidi! I'm pretty awake, too, so I'm really going to enjoy this trip!"

Then I felt another tug at the inner me, like something had a hold of my soul. I waited to see who was tugging and what it wanted. It tugged—again!

"Well, who is this?" I thought.

Then I thought to relax a minute and see what tingly vibes I might be getting from this tugging presence. I could already feel myself about to fly, as many do in their dream states and it's an undeniable feeling. So I felt I was starting to fly, but I couldn't get any "positive vibes" by whatever was near me.

I pressed on to feel it—and I did!

I felt almost as if a mask had been peeled back so I could now feel the dark presence behind this tugging and flying sensation! To be sure of what it was, I thought quickly to say Jesus' Name. Yet, once again my mouth felt filled with peanut butter motions. I also again refused to open my eyes to see the beast before me.

Jesus' Name finally left my lips and that's when I got the full reality of what was happening as I was dropped back down—unto my bed!

I didn't just have the sensation of flying, something was trying to lift me up—literally!

I felt that whatever it was, it grabbed me at the *exact* same points on both of my shoulders simultaneously and purposefully. As if it was only by these two points could this thing pinch, grab me and start to peel me from my body. I had both arms up and bent at the elbows with my hands curled towards my face (yes I sleep that way often). So when this presence grabbed me and started to lift me by the shoulders, my arms started to come up, too. It felt as if my shoulders and arms were only off from the bed a few inches before I got dropped.

The sneaky nature of this thing, where it didn't let on that it was even near, let me know that it was a coward trying a new tactic. With the timing of everything with this book being completed at the time, I felt it to be The Hat Man! After it let me go, I got up with such a strength in me while reciting the Lord's Prayer—I know that it was Jesus who stopped by, too! I walked around my entire place and let the dark presence know that I wouldn't slow down in putting this book out.

In knowing the threat of darkness in general, I know that the dark forces of The Hat Man are highly ticked off at me. But still, it was hard for me to admit that he got as close as he did to me. More than it is for me to admit that Jesus had stopped by—which I will gladly repeat at any time. ☺

Both of these incidences showed that we are all vulnerable, but all is not futile—not in the least!

Many people have ticked me off to want to at least tell them a piece of my mind at times, but I have yet to wish upon them that The Hat Man visits any one of them. If anything, when I see someone doing wrong, I'm actually worried that The Hat Man might catch their scent in the current and think of them as shark bait! So I am quite guilty of passing along warnings to people about him, especially if I caught a whiff of their rotten ways getting thick!

I can't help myself. But it's obvious that people who can harm him are also on his radar to attack them.

Another thing to note about a pattern The Hat Man follows, is that he is more likely to communicate verbally via ones dreams, rather than in-person. I came across a story via one of my Facebook groups that caught my attention about The Hat Man. The Hat Man appeared to this person in their dream, a dream that just so happened to take place right in their bedroom.

When he showed up, the question was posed to him, "Why are you here?"

Hat Man replied, first starting off in a whisper and ending in a growl of a scream, "Because you opened the door!"

For some reason, I can nearly clearly imagine what that might have sounded like! With a resounding understanding, it caused this person to awake in horror due to his growly outburst ripping through their mind into reality! It gives me the chills to even think of mouthing a whisper into a yelling voice like that! It also makes me wonder what "door" he was referring to and how it could be closed again—fully!

So again, it's a touchy subject to know of who is deserving of what. It's subjective and objective all at the same time, since The Hat Man is saying something took place in order for him to have shown up as he did to this person in particular. Obviously the person didn't know how or why he showed up; otherwise they wouldn't have asked him this question. But is there always a door opened for him to come through it?

I just can't smile at the fact to know that anyone, no matter how rotten, has experienced The Hat Man's glare. I like to think that there is hope for everyone to get away from his peering eyes and this is something I know is a real possibility. This life truly is what you make of it. For all I know, The Hat Man simply lied by saying a door was opened for him. Why would he reveal his hand to let you know that a door is opened that you need to close to potentially get rid of him? Then again, maybe he was instilling in his victim that he was invited somehow.

No matter what the circumstance is on why or how this Hat Man drug his ugly mug into your life, he's not in control of your destiny. As long as you have time on your clock, you can generate different outcomes up to the last minute. It's of course always recommended that you plan ahead and not try to cram change in at the very end! ☺

13

HAT MAN HANGING:

Keeping Bad Company

We have all had our down times when we feel that nothing is going our way where there almost appears to be no God who cares what happens to us. During these times we can become rebellious in character or reckless in our manners. We act like we care less than we should on what happens to us or even others nearby. But guess who shows he cares by showing up or simply pulling your strings to continue your downward-spiraling behavior?

That's right—The Hat Man!

The Hat Man might not always be easily seen, but his presence says it all. He can control how his presence is perceived with your eyes, soul, dreams, or your mood.

People are not always privy to catching a glimpse of him, in fact, at times it seems he prefers for his victims to not see who their puppeteer is pulling the strings in your life. Think about how The Hat Man shows up around death, illness, accidents and anything and everything that is less than positive, then you might see what I mean.

Dear Heidi,

I stumbled across your site tonight after having a talk at work with some people about Shadow People. Your site helped me to connect the dots to some events in my life that I had thought where disconnected. Let me start at the beginning:

As a small child I had "night terrors" where I would wake up and be fully unable to move. Sometimes I even felt like I was being levitated where I would be harassed by these evil bears. It all stopped abruptly when I got a stuffed bear that played the lullaby song "Frere Jacque."

I've had many emotional problems over the years and a few suicide attempts. It all came to a head when I was about 21 when I tried to kill myself. I ended up in the hospital for several days and I was diagnosed with having Bipolar Disorder.

I am 32 now and my emotional life has been very much under control. However, last year my wife got sick and it turned out that it was Multiple Sclerosis. For a time, she could barley walk and we didn't know why. It was perhaps the most emotionally intense and exhausting time of my life. It was during this time when I first saw the Shadow People with the one you call "Hat Man."

I think I made a mistake, though, because I challenged him!

I told him that he had no power and that his people were weak. The next night he appeared at the foot of my bed, but along side of him was the "Grim Reaper" form of Shadow. I didn't react, mostly, because the visit was very short. By the time I processed that they were there—they were gone!

About a week later I woke to find my bed surrounded by perhaps a dozen of these Shadow People. They took the shape of what you called their "true form," which is the humanoid figure with shoulders and red eyes (Head & Shoulders Shadows). Now, they have appeared to me several times since.

They seem to be smiling!

Not that I can see their mouths, but I feel them smiling—if that makes sense. What I find most disturbing is that when they appear, I have odd dreams. In these dreams I do things where I hurt people, animals, or myself. At first I believed they were trying to push me to hurt others, but I'm beginning to believe they are trying to push me into killing myself!

They come 1 - 3 times a week now. I have been praying more then ever before, but I'm not sure what else I can do. I hope that you may have something to suggest.

Right now I feel eyes on me. I feel that they are angry. I'm sure I will see them tonight, but I had to turn somewhere for help. I haven't told anyone what has been going on, not even my wife.

People often still refer to The Hat Man as "Shadow People." Again, this was due to my early assumptions in trying to define the various negative forces at the time. But now, you and I know better.

If you (the reader) knew The Hat Man to be the source as to why you and your spouse kept arguing over every little thing, maybe you would make a joint effort to show The Hat Man the door. If you knew why you woke up every morning with no energy, no dreams, no love and no drive—I bet you would find the right disinfectant to spray The Hat Man with! But if you haven't a clue that he is even lurking around scratching up foul moods of any sort, you would just sputter around allowing him to do as he pleased.

In regard to the email above, the first mistake was indeed that this man should have not challenged The Hat Man. Second big mistake is that he didn't tell his wife. All too often people try to go it alone, when apparently even The Hat Man needed his buddies to join him in oppressing this poor guy and his wife. If The Hat Man was powerful enough to take this man down on his own, he would have. Why go through all of the trouble to put a call out to the Grim Reaper looking guy and the Head and Shoulders Shadows?

It's because he *had to!*

This person needs to get his prayer buddies in order then, too. First he needs to tell his wife, then tell his friends to pray for him and most of all—talk to God more often!

It's bad enough to have one baddie show up, but this guy got an army of crappy comrades! That also tells me that this person must be a formidable enemy for these beings to put so much effort into taking him down! It's also apparent that they somehow had a connection to the somber mood and devastating diagnosis his wife was given. They were down and out, and these things approached? Perhaps they were already there breaking her down physically and then attacked outright after she and he both were weakened.

There's lots to ponder and so much to consider when it comes to The Hat Man...

Dear Heidi,

I hope this email finds you well. I'm writing to you because I have seen The Hat Man a few times. Most

recently, I saw him when I walked into my bedroom at 2:00 AM after getting off from work. When I came into my bedroom I saw him standing beside my husband as he slept!

I was startled and turned on the light immediately. I asked my husband if he was asleep and he replied, "No, I can't sleep because something keeps tapping my shoulder!"

I was very scared and proceeded to explain to him what I saw standing next to him. I have not read your book yet on Shadow People (*The Secret War*), but I hope to do so very soon. I'm contacting you, however, because around this same time last year the same figure showed itself along my house's outer wall and fence for a few days. I'm including the picture for you to see the side view of his face along the fence.

With the clear appearances of The Hat Man that I have witnessed, along with it comes this extremely negative and mean character that takes over my husband! Could there be a connection? I have included the sighting from last year - the side view of his face is on the fence.

I also wanted to tell you that I'd purchased a used piece of furniture and asked that it be delivered to me by the seller. Fortunately, that worked out and the man brought over the piece of furniture. However, as he walked into my home the hair on his arms stood straight up and he said, "The Enemy resides here!"

He claimed to be a preacher and did some intense praying for my husband and home to be released of this "enemy." He then told me that my life would change after that day. He said that I would be under attack by the enemy and to keep my Faith strong, because it would be angry that we were trying to get rid of it!

I have to admit that since that day, my husband has become a lot more calm and rational. He seems to have lost the hostile posture and aggressive demeanor he'd had for a long time. In fact, since that same day, my husband came home in a peaceful fashion and he has remained that way!

As the preacher man drove away from the driveway, I heard a loud crash in my bedroom. I walked over to see what happened and a shelf that held our wedding picture and my three children's baptism pictures—all had fallen to the ground! A few days later, a heavy-metal cross that was mounted in the hallway, fell and almost struck my youngest in the head as he ran past it.

Sometimes I feel like a crazy person discussing my experiences, but I do think something is here. All three of my children have been afraid of dark shadows in the hallway. My oldest claimed to see the "devil" and "demons" in my bathroom. He said this at the age of three when those words were not even part of our vocabulary in the house. The youngest described a red monster with horns and a big belly button at the same age of three and till this day he is hesitant to use that bathroom if no one is close by. At the age of four, my daughter claimed that she heard whispers in her room all night.

As you can see I've had several experiences and more still that I've not shared...

Fortunately, The Hat Man is flawed and can screw up where he gets seen or even photographed when he least expects it. However, it's not always that he's messing up, though. Just as you read here he was tapping on this man's shoulder to get his attention and perhaps get some respectful fear out of him, or at least disrupt his peace.

Yet, there are times when I am certain The Hat Man prefers he wasn't seen, but he has no choice in the matter. It seems that a lot of things that weren't so readily seen before are now being seen on a regular basis like spirit orbs, rods, lake monsters, Shadow People, ghosts, UFOs and other non-human creatures. There always seems to be something new getting reported or photographed in the world that's getting our attention to look further and think of other possibilities living within our reality.

The Hat Man does still intend to be seen by some of his victims for the notoriety and recognition he's craving, as mentioned. That can be easily determined by some of his actions like sitting on someone's bed, leaning in close towards someone and tapping, or jumping on someone. But then there's instances when he's hiding in someone's closet and the victim gets a sense of someone watching them. Then by chance they get a glimpse of The Hat Man in there as he reacts by receding—that's when I'm certain that he's goofed! However, sometimes when that happens, The Hat Man owns up to being present and takes a step forward to try and get the victim to recede instead of him.

But when he wants to be made out, he knows how to do it. Yet, there are those times when he's not appreciating the surprise of other's watchful eyes. I think it's fitting that he gets the table flipped on him when he thought he could pull the tablecloth off without disturbing anything like he's a magician or something. I know, another analogy—but such a fitting one!

Some of the times he's seen walking away (now that I'm thinking on it more), The Hat Man may not always be on top of his game. Possibly, some of his pointed camouflage is being broken when he starts to walk and witnesses get to see his tail-end whisking away. If someone intends for you to see them, so you can deal with them and address them, they would walk towards you and not away. Another interesting trend I've found is, when The Hat Man is seen walking away it's more often during the daytime and outside of people's personal bedrooms. So it does indeed sound like his hiding game is not as well thought out during these instances.

It seems that our watchful souls are capable of alerting us to his presence at a variety of times that something evil is nearby—lurking. What a neat trick God has installed inside of us.

Dear Heidi,

I recently had an experience with a vision of a "Hat Man". I did not know that was who I saw until speaking with a friend the next day about the vision.

It was a Sunday night and I was awoken by a strange sensation/vision in my mind that a man was closely standing outside (on my porch facing North) my kitchen sink window. I saw him as he left heading North or disappearing off the porch.

I am a big "chicken" but somehow I was okay to get up and go downstairs in my basement to do the laundry. I had to switch out the load of clothes and I looked out of the window as I went down the stairs. I got the sense of a presence being there, but I didn't see anything directly.

I never felt him to be good, but certainly not Satan, nor an alien. My sense was that he was a bad spirit or entity that watched me. I am not sure if he is gone, nor what he wanted. He looked like he had on an old fashioned Groucho style, pinstriped suit. He had a red carnation flower in his pocket, a white pasty face, thin mustache and dark hair, with a dark fedora style hat.

If a noted sense of gloom or negativity is lingering in your life or home, it's not always just the way life is. The Hat Man may get spotted orchestrating it all at times, or at least at some point. But there is no guarantee that you will get that chance if he can help it, unless he shows himself purposefully. But perhaps after he gets a better grip on you or needs to create a fear spot in your soul, he just might peer directly within sight. Just know that he is watching us all and is always looking to put his fingers where they don't belong.

Dear Heidi,

I had been confused about his appearance. I couldn't determine if he was real or a figment of my imagination. He appeared in my bedroom and just watched me. Me being me—I attempted to get up and defend myself. My problem lied in the fact that my feet and arms felt as though they had been bound.

My father was in the shower, but my mouth was sealed shut by thin air—just like my arms and legs were!

The only part of my body able to move was my torso. As I struggled to free myself away from these invisible bonds I closed my eyes to concentrate on them. When I opened my eyes again, he was gone! It seemed almost as if it were merely a dream, except my father was still in the shower and everything was in the exact same position.

Ever since this incidence, I get these odd, indescribable sensations.

It's as though something is touching only my brain and then dark intentions come forward. These intentions seem fully foreign, as though they don't belong to me! But they are successful in completely filling my head until the odd sensations are gone.

This story clearly shows how The Hat Man ignited negative thoughts to flow throughout this person's mind—though they were unwilling! Luckily, there's still a strong sense of this person remaining where they know the thoughts are not their own. My feeling is then, if that's the case, then they can also rid themselves of this thought provoker—The Hat Man!

Being at a low point in your life where you feel negative and others are being negative around you can bring your level of energy down in every way imaginable. It's like hanging out with the bad kids at school who pass on some drug habits to you and then you resemble your friend's downward spiral. Negativity feeds off from negativity and so does The Hat Man.

Just as the lion prefers to have an easy hunt for a fast meal. The lion goes after the weaker, less mature, more feeble, older and isolated antelope to pounce on. Why go after the strongest of the herd who can defend themselves best against an attack? That's a whole lot of extra work for the lion when the meat tastes the same! So recognize the acts of this lion, The Hat Man, who is aiming to isolate you and make you weak to his approaches as he watches you from your closet in hopes you'll fall when he's near.

The awful part is, we all will die at some point, that's just the way it goes. As my dad always says, "You aren't going to get out of this life alive!"

But how awful would it be that this angel of darkness is waiting nearby to grab you before anyone else does? That is an awfully scary thought! That's why the company that we keep is SO important, so we don't entertain The Hat Man to get comfortable enough to make an impression in our minds or souls.

There also is a risk taken for those of us who do what I call "fence sitting."

These are the people who choose to not make a decision or take a stance on where their heart and soul is when it comes to literally serving the interests of God. Before you start to attribute what I just wrote as me meaning that you have to be someone who is on bended-knee in prayer all of the time- asking God if you should take a step to the left or right—pause that thinking for a moment. I'm angling more on the notion that we as individuals think bigger than just ourselves.

So when it comes to taking a step to the left or right, is it to maintain something that is for good? Or, are you doing things that are only to fill your needs, though it might put someone at a disadvantage even if they don't know it? There's so many levels about what I'm aiming to get at here that it kind of simmers in my mind to ask this, "If you feel the pain of others and do you care enough to?"

We can't be a serial killer and then be the best son a mother could ask for. There can be no filter to where kindness and consideration is placed, because there would be a recognition that we are all connected and thusly hurt ourselves when we hurt anyone. Fence sitters distinguish and plan when they will be good and to whom and for what purpose. They are basically flip-flopping souls with a lot of potential, but ample opportunity for things like The Hat Man to make plans for them.

None of us are immune to his approaches, but some of us are more vulnerable than others.

Oddly, the talk of us living in the "end times" is abound and trending as often as Hollywood gossip is. One of the ways I see this as being evident is that not only is The Hat Man showing up exponentially, but sightings of Jesus are also WAY up!

Are the commanders of opposite armies checking up on their potential recruits? When Jesus shows up, trust me, that person is forever changed— never to doubt the power of God and their Faith in Him. When The Hat Man shows up, people are forever in fear that their souls may be in danger as their reality now realizes the real power of evil.

Two sides of the fence are being revealed and it's important to make sure your closet is literally cleaned out and there are steps to take to make it and keep it that way. We all have a choice to make on which way our personal efforts will go in this war we all know is coming at some point. So why not make a point to be ready for it if any of us are around for the big showdown, or at least for our own demise that is guaranteed to occur...?

14

ODD PATTERNS AND ENCOUNTERS:

A Lumping Of Horrific Stories

I have received so many stories about this Hat Man, I decided to delve back into this book just prior to it's publication to pop-in another chapter filled mostly with just stories sent to me over the years. There is so much diversity among the stories sent and I want you all to get a raw feel of the magnitude of what is in front of us. I also didn't feel that it was fair that I just sit on this information with no outlet for your discernment.

I feel like my soul is literally crying out sometimes to warn people and I hope this book and these stories make your soul want to scream out your own warnings to others, too. My thought is, if it helps, then it should be yelled—or told anyhow and somehow ☺.

Here's a lumping of stories that shows an undeniable pattern that The Hat Man likes to essentially, "tip his hat" in acknowledgment of those who see him:

HAT TIPPING STORY #1

Dear Heidi,

I have a story that I would like to share with you and yours.

This story took place in the Fall of 2008 around October. I was up late playing some video games when I got hungry. So I went downstairs into the kitchen to make a sandwich. On my way through the living room towards the kitchen, something in my subconscious nagged at me. I felt pulled to go and have a look out of the sliding-glass door in the living room.

So, I flung open the big curtains and had a look out at the night's sky. I stood in awe for a moment, gawking at the stars beaming through the trees. And then I saw him! The encounter lasted no more than 45 seconds, yet in my mind—it was an eternity! It felt like HOURS passed in those mere moments.

He didn't really just appear out of thin air. It was more like he just stopped blending-in with his surroundings. It was as if he simply stepped out of the darkness and into a spectrum of light that made him visible to my eyes. It reminded me of the alien from the movie "Predator." But instead of bending light around themselves, this Hat Man was able to somehow project darkness to camouflage himself.

As he "stepped' into my visual field, I was able to get a good look at him. He stood to be about 6 feet 2 inches and he had no facial features, or eyes. I could not make out any kind of suit on him. Plainly visible were the shadowy outline of his trench coat and his trademark Fedora hat.

I saw him and he saw me. In fact, I could FEEL him seeing me!

It was as if he had opened up my brain like a filing cabinet and was perusing my thoughts and memories to catalog for future reference. Almost like he was trying to size me up and understand what I was capable of. Perhaps even to determine what kind of a threat I might pose. In that one moment, I knew he was able to truly see and know everything about me!

Yet, during the first 30 or so seconds I did not feel any fear. No sense of terror came over me and I figured the worst thing I could do was panic. I think that a lot of my lack of initial terror stems from the self confidence I have gained studying martial arts. During these first few seconds, what I was seeing did not represent a threat to me, or perhaps my subconscious.

It was during the final 5 or 10 seconds that he took his step!

He took one, six foot, stride step towards the sliding-glass window that I was standing behind. It surprises me to this day that I did not get brown boxers as a result of this step. I took one reeling step backwards, away from the glass door, in absolute horror! I was very shaken by his big step towards me!

As I stepped backwards I exclaimed out loud, "Jesus H. Christ jumped up and played the fiddle."

Upon hearing me utter this admittedly silly quote, he stopped mid-stride! Then quickly, he settled back into balance and tipped his hat at me. As he tipped his hat, he took a shallow step backwards and once again ceased to be in the visible spectrum.

I continued towards the kitchen, in what could be best described as a state of shock. I made my sandwich and went back up to my room. The true fear I felt did not hit until after I had finished eating and had time to think about what I had seen.

"What WAS that? Or perhaps WHO was HE?" I would think to myself. The more I thought about these kinds of questions, the more the image of him standing there was burned into my subconscious mind.

A few weeks later, I was farting around on the Internet and tried to type in "Ghost fedora hat." Which got me a lot of spammed ghost videos and online fedora hat vendors. I then tried "Shadow Hat," which pulled up the term "Hat Man" on the Shadow People Wiki page. I was shocked to find a picture of The Hat Man entity I encountered staring back at me from the monitor. He was listed as one of the two most common shadow entities, with the other being "Head and Shoulders" (both terms of which I now know you founded).

I had chosen to not really tell anyone about this, because I didn't want to look like a loon. But after looking at your website recently, I thought this might be an account you would be interested in reading and posting.

What a daring and happenstance encounter with The Hat Man! We all live a life of routine where we just go about doing our thing, like grabbing a sandwich from our kitchen. It's sort of hard to anticipate, let alone imagine that one's soul may be challenged for the taking while in midstream of our routine—isn't it? But it happens. I cannot help but to wonder what becomes of the person who doesn't shout Jesus' Name out in some form?

It's kind of funny what this person said, it's a phrase I've personally never heard of before. Whatever it meant to that person, or simply that he said Jesus' Name, at least this action got rid of the threat heading directly for him. Jesus got the message, that's all that matters.

HAT TIPPING STORY #2

Dear Heidi,

I'm 35 years old and I only recently did a search online to see if I could find any info on something that happened to me when I was 6 years old:

It was a warm Summer's night, where I only had a tee-shirt on. My granny and her neighbor were outside chatting together on the pathway between their two houses. I think it might have been about 10 PM at night.

The front doors to both houses actually faced each other, with a square-paved area that had a metal railing running in the middle of it to divide it. I was swinging on the railing and playing while they continued to talk.

All of a sudden, this shadow of a tall, thin man appeared. He was wearing a top hat, a long cape and he carried a stick of some sort. He appeared at the very beginning of the paved area simply out of nowhere!

Then he just tipped his hat at us and walked straight between my granny and the neighbor! He then just continued to walk through the doorway of our alley that led to the back garden.

I felt that I must have been the only one to see him appear, since my granny and the neighbor just continued to talk. He obviously knew that we were there, since he tipped his hat in a polite and friendly manner. I didn't feel frightened by him and he didn't come across as evil or anything.

But, probably if it happened to me now as an adult I'm sure I'd be scared senseless! He had no facial features, but you could tell that it was a man. It was a dark night, but he was an even darker shadow. This happened in the 1970s in Northern Ireland and its not something you grow up talking about—so I didn't. Now as an adult, I've only shared this with others who are open to this sort of thing.

This hat tipping motion is an odd thing. It's done in acknowledgement and in an almost conceding manner of, "Well, ya caught me! So, I'll be on my way now."

Continuing on with more distinctive stories of The Hat Man. He apparently isn't a stout or short man. People have described him as being truly quite a sight to see, besides him being creepy as hell! But also because he's unnaturally tall:

TALL HAT MAN STORY #1:

Dear Heidi,

Just a few years ago I had a strange thing happen. I was living with my dad at the time and I'd just put my daughter to bed. Sometime during the night, I suddenly woke up. I didn't check to see what time it was though.

I laid there for about an hour trying to go back to sleep. I was looking out of my window, when I decided to roll the other way to get comfortable—that's when I saw him!

He was standing at the foot of my bed—The Hat Man!

He looked just like the classic description of him, too: Fedora hat, trench coat and shadowy—but two-dimensional! The closest thing I can compare him to is the monster from the movie "Jeepers Creepers!"

This Hat Man I saw didn't have any visible eyes, at all. The most impressive thing about this Hat Man is that he was HUGE!

The bed that I own has a top rail that stands to be over 7 feet tall. Imagine, this Hat Man was SO tall, he could have easily rested his chin on that rail!!! Actually, he might have had to stoop down a little bit to do that! So I estimate him to be 9 feet tall to the top of his hat, give or take.

The other thing that really stands out in my mind is the fact that he was standing right in front of my closet. My closet doors are made of mirrors and he DID NOT cast a reflection! It's funny, you don't think you would remember something like that, but you do.

Unlike most other stories I have read though, he did not fade away as soon as I looked at him. I stared at him for about a minute and I don't even think I blinked, because I was totally terrified. My first thought was to go get my daughter and get the hell out of that house! But I was afraid that if I ran for my daughter's room he would follow me and I didn't want him in her room. To be totally honest, I didn't really want to turn my back on it, either.

So I just lay there staring at him until I had to blink and in the split second it took me to blink, he was gone! The closet doors were still closed; my bedroom door was still closed. There was no other way out of that room, so I don't know where he went. I have never had anything like this happen to me before this and I have never seen him again.

In retrospect, I didn't really get the impression that he was there to cause any harm. I just think he was watching me. A few months later I met my husband and we were married less than a year later. I have read that some people see The Hat Man right before life changing events, so maybe he was visiting me because I was about to meet my husband? I don't know. I have only spoken of this to my immediate family, my husband (who has also seen a red eyed hat man) and the neighbor that lives across the street from my dad's house.

It's nice to know that I am not alone in this.

TALL HAT MAN STORY #2

Dear Heidi,

I read an article about this Hat Man online and I couldn't believe it! My son and I both were having bad dreams where we kept seeing this man appear right on our land. He was a seriously tall man, probably 7 feet tall, wearing a long black cape and a big black hat. We both dreamt of him appearing on the hill just behind our house.

He always had a deep, horrible voice and we could only see blackness where a face should be. I got a bunch of crucifixes blessed and put them above each doorway. It wasn't until we finally moved is when the dreams stopped!

The thing is, he didn't only appear in my dreams. He actually showed up in my bedroom one night and it was terrifying! I'd say it was one of the worst experiences of my life.

Trust me when I say that I'm not crazy, LOL!

Everyone always says he's a "tall man." But I never suspected he was abnormally tall until people started giving me actual measurements. Usually, people will say he's between 6 to 9 feet tall!

These next stories kind of blend in with The Hat Man being an abnormally tall guy. But he also seems to cast off more than a disturbing vibe. To some who see him, he doesn't seem to maintain his shape fully. He in fact seems to create a weird kind of distortion around him that appears more alien than paranormal:

DISTORTED HAT MAN STORY #1:

Hey Heidi,

After doing some research, it seems to me that all roads lead back to you regarding this phenomenon...

My boyfriend has been seeing shadows a lot lately, actually, for the past few years. Shadowy figures, blobs, smoke—he's been seeing everything. The other night I was sitting on my patio by myself smoking a cigarette. When I stood up to go back into my apartment it felt like someone was watching me. I looked to the side and there he was watching me over my fence—The Hat Man!

To stand on the ground and still have his whole head over the side of my fence tells me that this "person" must have been around 8 feet tall!

He was black and somewhat solid, but with yellow eyes! His eyes were actually glowing, but at the same time, they were what I would consider the opposite of light. It was like his eyes had the power to draw you in.

He was wearing a dark brown, fedora hat and had the appearance of static electricity all around his head. Then, I was suddenly seeing him in "tunnel vision." The strangest thing is that he didn't disappear and I wasn't afraid of him. The next thing I knew I was back in my apartment without knowing how I got there!

This situation has caused me to re-evaluate some situations in my life. When I was about 9, a friend of mine had an Ouija Board that her and I would play on. Everyday after school, we would sit for hours and speak to two entities that gave the names "Cat" and "Dell". They would joke, tell stories, and were very clever. They knew things about me I had never told anyone.

One told me that he was my guardian, that he was always with me and he would never let anyone get close to me because I was "his!" He answered questions I would ask only in my mind, leading me to believe it was not my friend playing some sort of trick on me.

For years I had a paralyzing fear of being alone in my room at night. I could feel a presence, a terrifying presence and extreme temperature drops. I can do nothing but draw parallels. I have also been experiencing extreme "haunting" type situations throughout my entire life.

About a month ago my boyfriend woke up in the middle of the night and found a large pool of blood on our bathroom floor with no tracks leading in or out! Like someone had been standing in front of our mirror—just bleeding! The next night I felt someone touching me in bed, then heard someone scratching at my blanket.

The list of experiences go on and on. The feeling of it all is decidedly negative and sometimes terrifying. As a note, the blood and touching began the night I received some holy water in the mail.

It's rare that I hear of The Hat Man wearing different colored clothing—but it happens. But did you pay close attention to some of the finer details of this Hat Man's eyes? This is quite rare, but I've had a few stories over the years claim that he had yellow eyes. With the boyfriend having seen the Shadowy things and her haunted background, shows there's lots of ties going on here to The Hat Man.

Some other interesting bits in this email tell of the obvious distortion of "static" around his head. Then she doesn't recall how she got back inside of her apartment and later her boyfriend found a pool of blood. These bits sound more alien to me. People have found blood with no source due to alien abductions, have missing time and not knowing how they got somewhere and some have seen odd static in the air or around alien creatures.

Question is: If this "man" that showed up is an alien, why is he aiming to look like The Hat Man? Or perhaps, is The Hat Man an alien?

Answer is: It doesn't really matter since they all get dealt with in the same way. Darkness is darkness. Light beats darkness—any day of the week!

DISTORTED HAT MAN STORY #2:

Dear Heidi,

I feel better that at least I can get this off my chest even if nothing happens more. I must give you a heads up, though, my writing is atrocious and I am basically typing out a stream of consciousness here with no editing. I wanted to get this out as fast as I can since I am detailing here what I saw and letting you know what my interaction was on all levels.

Here are the so-called bullet points:

Regarding my experience in 2004:

It had been a couple of days since we got back from Japan for my father-in-law's funeral. That night, I woke up at around 3 AM. I was in a state of paralysis and felt an unnerving feeling. Actually, I became outright fearful when I saw something in the corner of my room. It was a tall, black figure, about 7 feet tall with a brim hat!

I didn't see any arms, or the arms were at its side. It looked like it was wearing a trench coat, but I saw no detail. It was blacker than any area of the room and the room was dark. It seemed to shimmer on the outer edges of the silhouette, kind of like cheap special effects from a 70's TV show.

As I was staring at this figure I felt increasingly frightened where all of my senses felt like they were on fire. I actually shouted within my mind to get out and tried to challenge it to leave but I couldn't move. I tried to speak, but couldn't. So then I prayed to God to help me (even though I'm not religious and I don't go to church at all). My praying didn't work, that is, not until I used the Name of Jesus to help me!

Then suddenly, a short (3-4 feet tall) white figure materialized on the right side of my peripheral vision. It literally came out of the wall that my head was against and it had an odd walk. It seemed a bit hunched over like it was pushing something out of the way. As it walked towards The Hat Man, The Hat Man disappeared right along with the white being following it through.

The walk of this white being was very distinct, hunched over, using its hands to push something. It reminded me of a mime that pushes on a make-believe wall. But both of its hands were going back and forth with its palms straight out. All this while, the white being was moving extremely rapidly.

After this happened, I was free to move again! I got up and felt at ease since right away, I felt like someone had saved me from this Hat Man creature.

Recently, my Daughter (now 4 years old) has also seen this Hat Man without me saying anything to her. She told me she saw a dark man and then I asked her to draw it for me. To say the least, I was shocked and astonished of what she drew on the paper. I'm not sure if I have the paper still, I may have thrown it away. However, it was the same thing I saw in my bedroom years prior.

She said she saw a dark figure in our backyard by the pool. She said it jumped over the child protection barrier that surrounds our pool. Then it hovered over the pool a few inches and it shimmered or vibrated really fast and disappeared into the water!

My little girl has seen shadows and orbs at certain times during the day, off and on. One time we were sitting at a restaurant during the day and she went into some kind of trance and was staring outside the window. When she snapped out of it she told us she saw quite a few differently sized Shadow People standing outside. It kind of creeped my wife and I out a little bit.

Things got to be bad at one point with my sleep being interrupted by the dark presence. Plus, my wife and I felt we were going through some unusual bad luck during these times from the time we bought our house back in 1998. My wife's father and brother died within a 2-year period, suddenly. A couple of beloved pets died suddenly in the house, financial difficulty hit us all at once, and more.

We had always felt some kind of weird presence in the house. So we had a shaman we knew, come over to cleanse the house. Things have been better ever since then.

By the way, I am not crazy.

How wild that this person made the distinction on how their prayer didn't work—UNTIL they used the Name of Jesus?! I've got the greatest respect for other beliefs out in the world to keeping negativity away, but when it comes to The Hat Man, Jesus is the ONLY One I know who beats The Hat Man when called upon. I don't think the little light being that showed up was Jesus, but he obviously worked for Him. In my book *The Secret War*, I mentioned how beings who work for God don't look like the typical angels always imagined. It's been my experience that some of them can look quite alien, so reality is often stranger than our imaginations and artist interpretations of angels.

As mentioned before, The Hat Man likes to invoke negativity as you read in the prior email. But what do you suspect could be the worst of these negative vibes if they could form thoughts? Suicide. Which must be the worst of the darkest emotions known to mankind. The scary part is, some of the people who are taking their lives may not always be the one in control of their actions—to any extent:

UNDER HAT MAN'S CONTROL-STORY #1:

Dear Heidi,

I heard you last night on Coast to Coast AM with George Noory and I found what you were talking about to be very interesting, especially the part about "Hat Man."

About 6 years ago before my wife and I met, she tried to commit suicide by taking a whole bottle of pills. She says that she doesn't really remember what happened until she woke up in the hospital. The odd part is, her dad found her on the floor and said that she kept repeating about a "man in the hat" talking to her.

To be honest I never thought about it much. I just figured since she took a bunch of pills, that she must have been hallucinating. However when I heard you talking about "Hat Man" last night, I must admit, I got goose bumps! The thought of her suicide was the first thing that came to my mind and I just knew it to be true.

I just thought you might find this story interesting. It sure made me a believer of "Hat Man" after listening to you last night.

Oddly enough, only a couple weeks after reading this story to place in this book, I got a very similar story. This one came by way of a friend, though, which made it very personal. The same circumstance was played out, where a young person was found after having taken a large amount of pills. This person didn't recall doing that though, and in fact, they insisted that they weren't feeling depressed at all to even want to attempt suicide. But, this person had a past of seeing The Hat Man on a regular basis. You draw your own conclusions, but my friend and I listened to our guts on this one on who was responsible.

UNDER HAT MAN'S CONTROL-STORY #2:

Dear Heidi,

This story is one that I am ashamed to say. There was a time in my life when things felt like nothing could or would ever go right for me. So, I did the worst thing possible and attempted suicide by taking a ton of pills I found around the house.

I lost consciousness at some point and woke up in a hospital bed with my hands and feet strapped to the bed. No one was in the room, or so I thought. But when I looked at the chair pulled up next to my bed, there was this man wearing a hat and trench coat sitting in it.

He was creepy as hell when he smiled really nastily at me. Then he leaned in really close to my face and raised his hand to put his fingers out as if to show how big something might be in a pinching like manner. Then he said in a guttural-whispering voice, "I was this close to having you!" Then he disappeared in an instant!

I knew that he was there to take me to Hell if I didn't make it! I never wanted to even think of suicide after this happened—because I KNEW where I was going if I did!

The Hat Man doesn't always just sit by and let his minions do his dirty work. Sometimes, he likes to get his hands dirty. For anyone who actually gets touched by this Hat Man, it seems he is WAY too comfortable or has found a way at you somehow and this access should be denied. :

HAT MAN'S DIRTY HANDS-STORY #1:

Dear Heidi,

I heard an old interview you did probably three years ago that caught my attention because you mentioned The Hat Man and Shadow People. I would like to tell you of my experience and hope that it lends a greater understanding to this phenomenon. You may contact me, but I don't want anyone thinking I am crazy.

My parents, my sister and I, moved to a beautiful home in the 1980's in Arkansas. I was 19 years old at the time. The place used to be a farm where pigs used to be slaughtered and at least one suicide had taken place in the home.

To give you some personal insight:

My father is and always has been a very evil and mean-spirited man. Let me also mention here that my mother is the salt of the Earth. She is honest, innocent and a true, God fearing Christian.

One night in my bedroom I saw a black figure in a large brim hat with a cape. Like most scared kids do, I closed my eyes several times then reopened them hoping it would be gone. By the third time he was gone and I began hearing my mother mumbling in her sleep. I finally fell back to sleep.

The next morning I told my sister my unbelievable story. As I relayed it to her she physically turned white. She told me that two weeks ago my father told her that he had been woken up by a figure that matched the same description. But this Hat Man had my father by the throat and was physically strangling him!

This Hat Man had his knee buried into my father's chest as he strangled him, too! My father said this Hat Man felt like a lot of heavy weight was on his chest!

My father and sister had not told me about this prior, because they knew I would never have stayed in that house again. We told many people this odd story over the years and it still is very chilling to me! Many strange things occurred in the house following this event.

After this Hat Man encounter, I feel my father was never, ever the same. I truly believe he lost his mind after this "thing" visited him. My father was always evil and cruel, but never to the extent he was afterwards. My mom actually divorced him after 45 years of marriage. Something I never thought she would do, but things just got that bad.

My father revealed many years later that another entity visited him in that house and told him to write a book about the truth of Jesus. My father then told me of only a few of the details of what the thing told him to write. What little my father shared with me was so blasphemous that I told him to stop and that he had better pray for his soul!

I hope that this helps someone else who has seen this thing—not to feel like they are crazy. It exists and it is not nice, whatever it is.

When they get physical with their victims, choking a person seems to be a signature attack of The Hat Man and Shadow People. It has to be the most terrifying sensation to have something pounce on you out of nowhere in darkness and then attempt to strangle the life out of you! I've watched enough police dramas on television to know that when an attacker chooses strangulation, it's personal and they want to watch the terror in your eyes as you slip away into lifelessness.

More chills...

HAT MAN'S DIRTY HANDS-STORY #2:

Dear Heidi,

I was just on YouTube and heard a radio show you did about the Shadow People and The Hat Man. I guess I finally found someone to share my experiences with:

First off, I am an educated man with a great career and have nothing to prove to anyone. Nor am I seeking attention. I currently live in Southern California. I have nothing to hide and am willing to let you know who I am.

I just want to share and get some feed back from you.

OK, here we go...

Location: A friend's home in Arizona.

I was tormented by a Shadow Person in 1987. My older brother and dad also experienced crazy encounters with the same entity—so we moved. After that, we saw nothing. We thought it may have been just a poltergeist.

Occurrence: I met a nice one in 1992. It was a tall shadow man wearing dark clothes and a hat. He had no facial hair.

Location: Another friend's home in Arizona.

I had just arrived at my friend's home [about 5:30 PM] and as I was opening the door to get out of my car—I passed out. I was semi-conscious, but I remembered seeing a tall Shadow Man wearing a hat!

I'm not sure, but I think he hovered over the car and looked in through the windshield. I don't really remember how he got me out of the car, but I do remember him carrying me. I also remember entering the home—through a wall! My friends were home, but didn't see or hear a thing. They were in the living room and The Hat Man set me down by the dining room table. They eventually found me on the floor when they went to the kitchen to get something to drink [about 7:00 PM]. I don't know why I had passed out, but I do remember it was a very hot day so that may have been the reason.

Occurrence: In 1994, I literally fought and beat one up! This one looked old and had a very wrinkled face with an enormous nose. He wore a dark cloak and had red eyes.

Location: A friend's home in Arizona.

Time: Between 12:00 PM and 1:00 PM.

It was a very windy day and branches were falling off the trees. It's a common thing during the Spring so there was nothing to be alarmed about. Suddenly, I heard a flapping sound by one of the trees.

The sound was something similar to a flag flapping in the wind. Here's the thing—there were no flags in the area. As I was walking towards the front entrance of my friend's home the flapping got louder. Then I felt a presence coming towards me so I turned around quickly and looked up—there he was!

It was this scary looking man hovering over me, The Hat Man or Shadow Man. He literally picked me up and tossed me around a few times! Then, he actually spoke to me and told me he was going to take some of my friends with him. I didn't know where, but he seemed determined to do so.

I'm an experienced martial artist so I was doing everything to protect myself. I was not doing so well for a while, though. The altercation lasted about ten minutes. I was exhausted, but determined to make this thing get away from me! He never slowed down and he didn't seem to get tired. He also laughed a lot and called me a "young angel." I was mocked the entire time, so on top of it all, I felt very intimidated and overwhelmed.

Towards the end of the altercation, I heard a voice.

It was as if the wind was speaking to me. The voice told me to not be afraid and to believe in myself. It also told me that I was fully capable of making the man go away. The last thing I heard the voice say was, "Believe in yourself. You are strong enough!" It actually sounded like my own voice. Weird isn't it?

Anyway, at that moment, I felt a big boost of energy. I almost felt as if I could fly. I didn't though. The man had just thrown me across the yard into some trashcans, oddly, I felt no pain. Mind you, the cans were about 30 feet from where he grabbed me and threw me. As he approached me again, I turned to my left and saw the neighbors looking at us through their front window. I yelled at them and told them to get down. The man said that after he was done with me, he was going to take them!

When the man reached out to grab me again—I grabbed him! After I grabbed him, his expression changed. He looked scared. It was as if he had lost his strength. All of a sudden, he was asking me to forgive him, but something didn't seem right. I didn't really know what to do so I pushed him to the ground and he began to sink.

It was as if the dirt was turning to mud and it consumed him?!

The last thing I told him was that I was going to send him back to where he came from. I think I did. After that, the neighbors came out to check if I was okay. A few minutes later, we heard a splash and someone coughing by the right side of their home. We quickly ran towards the side of their home and found my friend. He was wet and had a gel-like substance all over his body! He told us he was okay and didn't know how he got there.

I really think this thing was an extraterrestrial being. As a matter of fact, I feel positive it was or is because he/it hovered. Currently, my friend is doing well. He's married and has a child. Sadly, the neighbors [mother and son] who witnessed the event have both passed away due to drug overdoses.

I've also had three encounters with tall large-headed lizard creatures. One of them was a child. I feel weird by talking about all of this. I really hope this info goes to the right person. I honestly feel that there is something coming. I've been dreaming [since the age of 5] of a war between us, them, and the Shadow People. But not all Shadow People will fight against us. When it happens, we will also witness the return of the T-Rex and other reptilian creatures.

In these dreams, the reptilian creatures come out from under the ground and mountains—not from outer space. The key is confidence and believing in our strength in numbers. Keep in mind that we are not just protecting ourselves.

We're also protecting our freedom.

I also dream of a robot war. I think that robots will be used to fight these things.

Does all of this sound crazy to you? I have a lot more to share, but I just want to know if you are interested.

HEIDI HOLLIS

Now this is a story that sounds like straight out of the movies, doesn't it? Like I'd be crazy to even put this story in this book as if it should be believed—right? Although this encounter is a unique one, it's not the only one I've received of beings similar to this one come swooping at them out of the sky! Why was this one so adamant in attacking this man, I couldn't tell you. I think the "nice one" he mentions actually is the one responsible for making him pass out in the first place. But I will tell you my insight into some clues shared here.

This person obviously has a history within their family of Shadow People and then personal Hat Man encounters. But what struck me the most, was this person's insight, visions or dreams of what I've called "The Secret War" (as mentioned is the title of my book based on the war between us, aliens and Shadow People)! There is a conflict at hand, there is something coming, and apparently this person is a threat of some kind. So much so, that they threw everything at him to shut him up and take him out! Darkness doesn't like to be found out and they surely don't want people around who might have some insight into a dark situation that is brewing.

I have to say though; I couldn't help but to think of the movie "Pacific Rim" when he mentioned the dinosaurs returning from the Earth. But I've always thought that Hollywood spoon-feeds us other possible realities to see if we can handle them or get the notion in our head. Then there is also the very real reason why some of these odd scenarios are made into film—someone else dreamt them up perhaps even literally!

By the way, I always find it interesting how people like to ask me if something sounds crazy to me or not. It never gets old! ☺

The Hat Man isn't one to talk a ton, but when he does it's very much to the point. I mentioned earlier that he generally speaks in people's dreams, but not always. Either way, when he does talk I try to pay attention to what's being said and why:

CHATTING HAT MAN-STORY #1:

Dear Heidi,

I affirm on my life that this is the whole truth. I have not left anything out, nor have I added anything.

I was 16 years old when I was incarcerated for getting into trouble as a youth. I was sleeping on the bottom bunk of the jail cell at the time. Out of nowhere, I was roused out of my sleep. So I sort of glanced around to see what was going on and to my right side I saw a figure standing in a long black coat with a hat.

I thought this was all really strange because, for one, I was in a locked jail cell that no one could enter! Secondly, I remember thinking that he looked like the Undertaker character from professional wrestling (WWE).

Then, I got a strange and daunting feeling that I was dying—like my heart was about to stop. He then reached out with his right hand and placed it on my chest. That's when I could clearly see this light coming from his hand that he was pushing into my chest!

Then, I heard the words, "Live your life." Just like that, he suddenly disappeared!

I am now 33 years old and to this day—I am still puzzled by this. I did not find out until recently that many people have seen him. So then, that must mean that he must be real, because we can't all be having the same dream!

Here someone who has been incarcerated for being negative enough to be locked-up, feels they are about to die. That's when new life gets breathed into them by The Hat Man (of all people), who pushes *his* light into them?! After reading about him from so many angles—what does that make you think?

I don't like to be the bearer of bad news, but my heart hurts every time when reading this one. I don't know if being rescued in this instance was the best thing to have happened. It's as if The Hat Man knew this person was about to die, came for the occasion and gave them his spark of life and tells them to live that life he's given them, now!

As with the story where The Hat Man picked up an unconscious man and now this jailed individual, some might think The Hat Man is not all that bad. Right? Trickery is also a trait of darkness. What may seem like a kind act, might only be a ploy for a person to let down their guard to allow him to be closer to them. Stories of his "acts of kindness" might also serve to confuse people who read of these acts of The Hat Man, too. But trust me when I say that these types of Hat Man stories are quite rare, so don't go around opening up yourself to this Hat Man in hopes you'll find a "nice one."

It reminds me of the abducting alien stories again, of people who have been trespassed upon by these abusive and deceptive aliens. But to some alien abductees; "their" abducting, raping, experimenting, Jesus hating, healing to be worshiped as "god" type of aliens—*are* the so-called "good guys?" Who only rape, experiment, heal to be worshipped, and run when they hear Jesus' Name—only do all of these things out of necessity for ours and their own good!

Well, that's a big, fat lie! Yikes! Did I just write that? I did.

Sorry, but that's my common sense perception—but you decide.

CHATTING HAT MAN-STORY #2:

Dear Heidi,

Of course, during this attack in this nightmare I'm about to share I couldn't remember it word-for-word. I just remember calling on St. Michael and saying the words, "Thrust into Hell!" Right when I heard myself say the word "Hell," the thing vanished! It just poofed out of existence immediately. Everything stopped and it was chilling.

When I finally woke up in Germany a few minutes later, I realized what had happened. My heart was pounding, hair standing on end and I had goose bumps all over for 5-10 minutes. Afterwards, I had the sneaking suspicion- almost like an imprint left behind—that this was the devil himself that I saw in my dream! On top of it all, I knew that this was punishment.

I got the message across to me that, "You belong to me! You're mine! I own you—don't forget that!"

Forgive the poor taste of reference, but it felt like a pimp beating up on one of his prostitutes for wanting to leave the industry. It seems that I always get a visit like this within a period of a few weeks when I make more of an effort to renounce him and follow Jesus!

I thought The Hat Man was unique to me. So, you can imagine how my jaw dropped when I saw what you said of him and read of other's experiences regarding him. This coupled with the things that have been going on in my life, including these horrid nightmares. Plus the suicide attempts coupled with a lifelong problem with depression and then I'm told, "You belong to me?!" Ugh!

I never wanted a spiritual battle. I never believed in God or the devil. I never believed in possession, oppression, curses, consecrations, or any of that. I mean shit—I feel like just by talking about it I need to check myself into a damned mental institution! I realize that fear feeds off fear, too.

Often, you can work your brain into such a tizzy, that the whole thing becomes self-perpetuating. I realize that putting yourself into a good mental state and happiness often gets rid of these things. Problem is, I've been surrounded by the darkness for my entire life it feels.

I reach out to God, but I feel He ignores me. I ask to know Jesus—He never comes. I ask Mary to pray for me and here is the real messed up part: Anytime I see or say Mary, the word "bitch" goes zinging through my head and I have zero control over it! It's blasphemous to the extreme and I was never raised this way—even personally find it appalling!

Literally, that is another one of the things that scares me to my core. I try not to talk about it. But, I can't pray or mention Mary without blasphemous things zinging through my head like that. It's like something else is in there with me saying these things! I think I might have much more serious spiritual problems going on within me than I previously could have ever imagined.

In fact, so long as you ignore it —it doesn't happen. If I ignore it and go about my life and pretend God doesn't exist and I don't give two shits—I get left alone. But when I start to try and fight it, I get hassled. That blasphemous voice I hear through my head is actually the scariest part and the part I'm most ashamed of. I honestly have zero control over it.

I'm not schizophrenic. I'm not psychotic. I'm not taking medicines. I don't hallucinate. I'm not crazy.

Did the impact of this person's story hit you hard, too?

It's no wonder why this person is depressed and attempted suicide—they are being manipulated by The Hat Man! This story is self-explanatory about what's going on and that they are being misled to believe they are the property of The Hat Man, because it's simply not true. How do I know this? The simple fact is, when this person called out for protection from one of God's workers—help arrived! There's always help to break free from the grips of this negative idiot—The Hat Man. Never doubt that, no matter how pushy he might get.

If this Hat Man was *so* in control of this person, then he wouldn't have to come to remind them about his control—now would he? He has to do a whole hell of a lot to keep making sure this person doesn't break-free of his grip. But it does seem like he's got something whispering in their ear of blasphemous things, nearly like a possession like the previous story. So I'd say this person needs to get that dealt with and have it tossed to the side.

It also never gets old being told how a person is not crazy for sharing their story with me. I don't see how it would be presumed I'd think that of them. Nonetheless, I often get lists of all the mental illnesses that could befall a person who might see such things. ☺

Also, The Hat Man can often step out from the shadows to reveal a side of him that few would ever want to experience. These are some of the more gut wrenching experiences I've received that will always keep a perturbed look strewn across my face and soul. Just when you think The Hat Man can't get any uglier, he goes and puts his ugly face on:

UGLY HAT MAN STORY #1:

Dear Heidi,

My story happened in Carcross Yukon Canada at a historic graveyard when I was only 5 years old. This graveyard has a deep rooted history during the times before the gold rush of white men who came to the area. Anyways, one night a bunch of us kids went running wild in the area just having fun. There was about ten of us when we decided to try and scare ourselves by going to that graveyard.

Everyone ran into the graveyard, but I refused to cross the threshold out of fear. I got teased for it and called "chicken," but I still didn't budge. I remember watching them taunt me while I felt an overwhelming sense that I was being watched. So I sort of looked around to see what I was feeling and my eyes landed on this entity at the edge of the graveyard, at the bottom of a hill!

The creepy part is, this thing was floating about 3 feet off from the ground!

It was all black. Actually, it was more like the absence of light. What was stranger is that I could make out the ruffled look of a cloak that it was wearing. It looked like the kind of cloak a stagecoach driver would wear in England during the 1700's!

I looked up at it from the ground-up, just like they pan a camera in a horror movie to reveal a horrible monster lurking about! As soon as I looked into its face, I locked eyes with it. His eyes were a deep red and I knew that he was looking at me. None of the other kids even noticed this thing being there.

As I continued to lock eyes with this thing, I took note of his top hat that was wide brimmed. The other feature that was horribly disturbing—was his smile! He had pure white teeth that were jagged like a piranha and his smile went from ear-to-ear!

The feeling I got from it was pure evil! Being a 5 year old child—how could I know what pure evil was? But I was certain of this man being evil as he locked his gaze onto me like a cobra, making me completely paralyzed.

Somehow, something finally allowed me to scream and point at it. This made the kids finally all turn around to see this thing headed our way. As they did, every kid ran past me leaving me behind still paralyzed with me pointing at it! My brother finally came back for me and drug me away completely stiff as a board, still unable to move freely!

To this day I *know* that I saw the devil!

I always felt that this Hat Man wanted to get a point across to me—almost like he was leaving his mark on me with his look! Being an artist, I've almost painted him several times. But I was afraid if I did that it would draw him to me again, so I never have even attempted to.

Throughout my life I have been almost plagued with strange things. I saw a UFO around the same age of 5. Since then, I am pretty certain that I've been taken by aliens. Sadly, I don't think there's much that I can do about this happening to me.

When I found out that you coined the term of "The Hat Man," I knew that I had to write you. I had never heard of red-eyed Shadows until I started researching it. Prior, I'd never heard of any of them wearing hats, until I saw your site. Suffice it to say, it's been very chilling and it's freaked me out to find that I'm not the only one!

The closest story to mine that I've ever heard personally was via a friend. He said he was camping in the woods and had to go use the toilet away from the campfire. He was looking at the ground as he walked towards the bathroom and spotted something from the ground-up. He first saw hoofed feet, then as he glanced upwards they were connected to goat legs. Then as he continued to look, the torso was a shadow and its face only shimmered red eyes!

He told me that all he could do was run and bolt past the camp as fast as he could. He jumped into his car, left everyone at camp and turned every light on in his house for days! He also claimed he saw the devil.

I had to share with you what I saw, because I'm sick of people rolling their eyes at me if I tell them! So thanks for your time...

Talk about an ugly Hat Man story—eh? I told you there were some nasty ones out there! What sort of sinister point can be embedded in a young child to know that somehow this beast of a man coming your way is looking to mark your soul? It truly turns my stomach in disgust.

I hope you are seeing that this Hat Man hasn't just waged a war on the most innocent who cannot readily defend themselves. When these innocent ones are targeted, it's a call to arms for *all* of us to stand guard. So no longer can we ignore the cries of a child that a "Bogeyman" was after them, under their bed or in their closet. For all we know, it just might be true!

So what would it hurt to say a prayer of protection with your child to make sure that thing they fear will stay away? Do it nightly if it keeps the child's soul protected and away from something that's compared to the likes of the devil! We can't be everywhere for every child, but we can arm them to know what to do in the face of evil. Start them knowing these things while they are young and build up their Faith from the start.

I will insert in here, as well. That there aren't enough people instilling Faith into their children's lives. If you haven't the time to go to your religious institution, then get some reading material to read with your children. I'm biased to suggest my graphic novel series (*Diary Blog of the Fickle Finders*), but as long as some kind of approach is done, that's what's important!

UGLY HAT MAN STORY #2:

Dear Heidi,

For as long as I can remember I've been tormented by this Hat Man being. I had my first encounters with him when I was a young kid of 3 years old. My entire childhood became his victim as he destroyed it. He's been such an ordeal to handle that I now prepare to battle him—even in the afterlife!

I feel that my life is under the influence of this Hat Man, so much so, that I feel it wants me to kill myself. I would of course never allow it that pleasure, but everything in my life goes from bad-to-worse no matter what I do.

This Hat Man even comes at me in my dreams and in-person. One time, I was out walking my dog when it appeared about 15 feet in front of me. The dog actually saw it before I did, then The Hat Man spoke and asked the dog, "What the hell are you looking at?!" I then looked to see him standing right there and he remained for about 8 seconds! Then I watched as it drifted into the ground sideways. It didn't fade, it just went into the ground!

I am certain now that he's appearing to my 3 year old son, because he's acting very much as I did when I saw The Hat Man at his age. So now, I want to know how to destroy it. Now he's in this taunting stage.

He's woken me up from sleeping and said to me while I was trying to wake up fully, "I'm a demon!" I shot straight up to confront him, but he just quickly walked away into blackness.

He was right in my face just like a drill Sergeant when he screamed this at me, too! When I opened my eyes, I could see this mangled flesh on his face with no real features. He looked humanoid, but like a burn victim without eyes, nose or even a mouth!

I think he knew that this tactic didn't scare me and that's why he ran away like he was actually scared that he had tempted me to get him!

Yes, apparently The Hat Man will even yell at a dog if he's so moved to.

What a wimp that he cannot handle the innocence of a pet protecting its owner? The dog then obviously created a barrier that he stopped to ask the dog a question! ☺ Kind of funny, I think anyways. Did you catch how he similarly went into the ground, as was mentioned in the story of the flying Hat Man who beat on a guy?

What was interesting in connection to this story and the one just prior is how The Hat Man will change his face to see if it will invoke some new fear into his witnessing victim. He purposely aims to instill a deep-rooted fear, but again, he rarely physically confronts a person outright. He appears to go at a person and then doesn't follow through on his threatening stance as he waves his ugly face at people to forever be engrained in their memory.

Then just as heard of before, this Hat Man is taking a look down the family line to this person's son. But just as most any parent would want to defend their child, this victim now is declaring war on The Hat Man. Physical threats isn't what keeps this vicious entity away, but putting the fear of God in him does—literally!

On to the next stories: When I first spoke of Shadow People, the link I made with them is how they have connections to aliens. I also mentioned that notion here and how The Hat Man is tied to Shadow People. So then that might suggest that there's an alien connection with The Hat Man, too.

Like I've said, darkness is darkness! It doesn't matter where it came from, or what you call it—it exists. It's like the saying, "Everybody poops!" It doesn't matter where the poop came from, all that's known is that it's undesirable and no one wants the poop in their presence.

Here are some stories that show people living with one foot living with the terror of The Hat Man and the other on a UFO somewhere:

HAT MAN ALIEN TIES-STORY #1:

Dear Heidi,

I started seeing The Hat Man at the age of 7. I would awaken in the middle of the night to see this tall shadow of a man standing there in a fedora hat and trench coat (or cape). He had no distinguishable features and was seemingly picking up "something."

For some reason, I vaguely remember it being a bucket he was picking up. Later on, my younger brother told me he saw a silhouette of the same man multiple times—also picking up something! He would fully paralyze me when I saw him. But the second I could

move, I would jump out of bed and run past him towards my parent's bedroom!

Every time my parents would come to check my room, nothing would be there. I then started to dismiss it as hypnagogic hallucinations and nothing more. Then one day, I looked up Shadow People online. When I saw the article on The Hat Man—my hair stood on end! That was because I'd then fully realized that this was not just a manifestation in my mind—but that he was real!

Now, I've become near paranoid that I might see The Hat Man again.

Over the past few days, I've actually caught things moving around the house and got some on camera! I even got some images that show this shadowy thing wearing a hat! Then I heard what sounded like a grunt or growl and it really freaked me out quite a bit. As I was snapping pictures of this thing, my camera suddenly stopped working. Then to make matters worse, my camera totally disappeared and I know I didn't misplace it!

I've also been seeing some preying mantis type creatures that are gray in color. What's weird is I haven't seen them directly, but more like lucidly in my mind or in a darkened room. There's even been a lot of paranormal activity going on around me lately. There just always seems to be an object getting moved on its own or my hearing faint voices and such.

What is truly striking and relating to having alien ties in this story, is the mentioning of these Preying Mantis type creatures. These beings are exclusively tied to the alien encounter phenomenon that gets reported globally. These beings are as cute as the gross, predatory bug we see around today snapping up other small creatures. They aren't looked upon as being pleasant creatures and are known to abduct as cruelly as any other negative alien. As mentioned earlier, negative alien beings are related to the Shadows and Shadows are seen alongside of The Hat Man. So once again it's a vicious, connected cycle.

HAT MAN ALIEN TIES-STORY #2:

Dear Heidi,

Okay, so I need HELP!!!

My brother was in bed just last night when he started hearing a "humming noise" that paralyzed him!!! Then, he saw a shadow man—The Hat Man. It was walking around the room casually, but kept going back and forth to his son's baby crib.

My brother couldn't move at all until The Hat Man left and then the humming noise stopped. He is extremely worried about his baby and what this thing might do to him since he couldn't even move to protect him.

Please help!!!

Is there anything you can suggest on how he can protect his son from this Hat Man?

The triggering similarity between The Hat Man and aliens in this brief, but explosive story is the "humming noise." People often describe hearing a high pitched, whining, buzzing or humming sound before and during alien encounters. The person is also rendered unable to move in the same manner upon hearing this sound, or know that something is about to happen when they hear it.

But it's important to note that The Hat Man, as well as aliens, can also paralyze people with just a glaring stare. The feelings of horror that come with being paralyzed is another common trait. Then there's the high interest in going after the children of experiencers of either phenomenon. Just giving you the full picture to look at here.

HAT MAN ALIEN TIES-STORY #3:

Dear Heidi,

What I experienced over a few weeks time about two years ago, has left me in awe. What happened even had me doubting myself because of the bizarre combination of events and things I witnessed. But after hearing how you've tied all of these odd occurrences together—I don't feel as crazy!

Over the years I've experienced a lot of odd things like hearing phantom sounds like footsteps or seeing things out of the corner of my eye. But starting a few years ago, I felt like a target for malevolent forces. I think it's partially because I've had a hard time fully accepting the Christian Faith because I feel it's become nearly corrupt on how it gets interpreted. Now I feel that I'm sort of owned by Satan so that I can be used to ridicule God.

One night I saw a girl with extremely long hair, covering her face. Her hair stretched to the floor and she was soaking wet—it was like a scene straight from the movie "The Ring!" As soon as it took a step my way, it vanished in an instant. Later that same night I woke up to find that the power was completely out in my room except for my alarm clock that was flashing "4:00 AM." My cell phone wouldn't even work! What's even stranger, if the power goes off and comes back on—the alarm clock will only flash 12:00 AM (doesn't everyone's)!

Just then I was filled with absolute dread and I turned to see my door crack open slightly. That was followed by long fingers coming through and two Grey alien heads peeping through! We locked eyes and they looked just as surprised to see me awake as I was to see that they even existed!

Then instantly—a light flashed and everything went black!!!

It nearly seemed as though I woke up all over again in the same situation as before: The power was off, the clock was flashing 4 AM, and I was filled with dread. The only difference is THIS time I turned over and there was a huge black mass, right where the Grays were the first time. But this thing looked like a wizard or a cloaked man! The guy was huge enough that his head touched the top of my 12-foot high ceiling!

All I could think to do was pull the covers over my head and begin to pray. Then I felt my bed sink-in as this thing moved over me from my legs to my face! It felt like it was fully sucking the air out of my lungs as I laid there paralyzed, but fully aware! I was sure that my heart would beat out of my chest wall as I tried with all that I had to fight it off!

Eventually, I guess I just passed out because the next thing I remembered was waking up in the morning. I felt ill and had a hard time breathing for the next several days. I didn't know what to make of any of it. I have to admit, that though I did tell people of the Shadow figure-that's all I mentioned. I always left out the part about the Grays because I felt like even that was too unbelievable! Not until I saw your website and research pairing up the Shadows and aliens, which made the hair on my neck stand up!

The evil experiences continued for the next week or two with other sightings of Shadows, feelings of dread, hot breath on my skin, rabid growls in my ears, being touched, mysterious power failures, and even a possessed toy robot (which is very peculiar considering your clown story). After I got my place blessed these things all stopped, for the most part. But I still cannot turn off every light in my room without hearing banging, footsteps and the sounds of objects moving around in my room.

I am certain that the Power of God keeps these things at a certain distance to tone them down. But I've learned that Satan can go anywhere, so I feel I cannot prevent them from at least making their presence known.

Have you ever heard of others seeing the Grays and the Shadows showing up simultaneously? The image of those Grays has burned in my mind even more than the giant Hat Man attacking me! I knew it really happened, but I had hoped it was only a nightmare.

I feel like things are about to get worse as if they are growing stronger. I never feel like I'm alone, like someone is hovering over me at all times. I am worried something is building up again and honestly I feel as if I can live with the intimidation of The Hat Man. But the thought of seeing the Grays again, for some reason, it scares me beyond belief!

I am hopeful that I can fully rid myself of all of these episodes at some point. It'd be nice to actually sleep a night in my adult life again, without having to have a light on! I'm also certainly concerned that I don't want to endanger my future family by these things.

I don't see how clearer it could be, with even just this one incidence, how darkness is related among these various beings. One would of course have to believe that this is a true and accurate account of what took place. It sounds sincere enough to me, but I will leave it up to you to decide—once again.

To address some of the concerns this person is going through, it sounds as if a "smoke-screen" of a memory might have been put in place of him seeing the Grays. So who put that memory there? Did the Grays not like that they got caught, or did The Hat Man take over to get the job done right since the Grays goofed by being seen?

In my experience, I encountered a whole hoard of Grays, only to have the Shadow People start showing up in my place nearly the next day. It was explained to me via a being named Cafth (see my book *The Secret War* for the full story) that since the little minions couldn't take me down and got seen—that they then sent their boss after me! I don't know if this is the same case or not, but it sounds awfully familiar.

Many who have experienced aliens, see ghosts, have psychic episodes, experience out-of-body trips, have poltergeist phenomenon, altered realities and the list goes on. It's not so cut and dry to try to figure out what's NOT related when it seems much easier to point the finger at what IS related.

I know how these sorts of stories can really leave a sense of heaviness when you read them. I've been drudging through them for years feeling the anxiety and anguish that so many are having to endure. So it's only fair to hear some of the tactics that have worked for people who have experienced this Hat Man—with the Power of Jesus! ☺

JESUS TO THE RESCUE-STORY #1:

Dear Heidi,

I've seen this Hat Man only two times, but that was enough! I was just a young girl the first time, so I wasn't really scared—more unnerved. I was kind of used to seeing odd things because I'd experienced angels, demons and all kinds of ghosts.

The second time I saw him, I woke up to see this Shadow Hat Man standing only a foot away from my bed! He was wearing a coat and hat on like he was from the 1940's-mobster times! Before I opened my eyes to see him there, I could sense that something was wrong. But for some reason I had a hard time waking up, only to find him staring at me.

He didn't seem to like that I woke up, so he kept putting me back to sleep where I felt drugged, somehow. I was fighting him so hard to stay awake and that's when he started getting really angry with me! He started calling me horrible names like "bitch and whore" and some other negative names. Then he made me think that he was going to put my bedroom dresser up against the bedroom door so I couldn't ever get out.

He literally started grabbing and pulling at my toes as he kept trying to put me back to sleep! This all happened at around 3:00 AM. I always had my belief in God, though I didn't know much about Jesus Christ at the time. So I took the time to call my mom and she told me a small prayer to say that would help and invoke the Name of Jesus—and it worked!

I must have fought that Hat Man for two hours before calling my mom, it was nearly daytime outside by then. This thing was SO evil—I KNEW it came from Hell!!!

Years later, I have seen other Shadows, but not with hats. The others also moved a lot faster than The Hat Man. I'm glad to say that now I'm a true believer of Jesus Christ! ☺ Not that I would want to fight with The Hat Man again, but if I had to—I am SO positive that he does not like the Name of Jesus!

What's interesting about this encounter is that The Hat Man obviously didn't like the fact that he got busted by this onlooker. So what might this be saying? Could it be that he does do the intimidation game on witnesses to scare the life out of a person so that they will be silent? At times it does seem to be one of the reasons. Then there's the times he purposely aims to wake a person, so his tactics widely vary.

What's most important to learn here is that it didn't matter about his reasons to want to hide this time around. All that matters is that his plan didn't work and his victim wasn't going to be victimized any further. Amen!

JESUS TO THE RESCUE-STORY #2:

Dear Heidi,

When I was in high school in 1960, I had a strange encounter. I woke up one night hearing footsteps coming up the stairs in the direction of my bedroom. I called out to see who it was, but no one responded. So I called out again. Before I knew it, a dark figure was at my bedroom doorway.

It stood there silently only for a moment. Then suddenly it started to approach my bedside. It looked like the same hat-ed (and hated) figure on your website—exactly!!!

I was absolutely terror struck and could not scream or move! Without a word this thing fell silently and directly on top of me! It was attempting to smother me!

I struggled to free myself and finally I was able to crawl blindly towards the light switch near the door. When the light came on-the creature was gone!

Was it a dream, an apparition, or a demon? I don't know! But during that time in my life I had a lot of vivid dreams of the world ending and meeting God on

a hillside outside of Denver. He comforted me and other frightened survivors as we watched the city burn and then become engulfed in a vast flood of water. I was scared but I was more than reassured by the being of glowing Light in a long robe.

He spoke in a wonderful and comforting manner. The real irony in the dream was that in the beginning, the city was evacuated in anticipation of a nuclear strike. When we reached the government built shelters, near Red Rocks, we discovered that they were never finished due to a lack of funding. We stood in a state of shock as the first flash of red light appeared on the horizon. I was so sure that this was going to happen that I refused to go to school for a week!

Here goes another person who is nearly engulfed into the pure evil of this Hat Man, but who had connections that ran deep with God in his visions. So was he someone The Hat Man wanted to silence? This person had more than one scenario given to them of what to do in case the end of the world took place and to have Faith that all would be okay. I would say that is one voice evil wouldn't want around to help encourage others during cataclysmic events—even happen stance ones. That sounds like a house call needed to be made—so The Hat Man made one!

This story should also show others who have experienced him, know that you aren't necessarily screwed because you saw him. He can be just as drawn to your light as he is to your inner darkness. But I would say that if he's making a habit of influencing your sleep to be restless, make you feel you are being watched, touched, given bad luck or anything daunting...then he's too damn close!

It doesn't matter why he's there, he's there and he needs to be shown the door out of your life and home. I hope this sampling helped dig you all a little further into the rabbit hole of mystery with me. We can and will defeat this guy, but let's not go it alone—agreed?

Good.

Then let's start educating each other about this threat so he doesn't gain anymore ground during his covert approaches of evil. Too many people suffer alone needlessly. It's time that stopped and you can all do your part by just opening up your mouths and minds a little bit more to educate people. You will be stunned how many people you will meet who just might open up to you about their own odd encounters they've struggled with.

Be brave, be strong and be mindful on how you react when you hear their stories, too. Because what you do could set the course of another's spiritual wellbeing in this life—and the next! Let me know if I can help, too. Write me via my website and I will do my best to lend some advice. ☺

15

NO WELCOME MAT:

Closing The Door

Seeing anything coming ones way that is even slightly resembling the likes of the devil, is not a good thing no matter how it gets looked at. If a person is able to get up and look the devil in the eye and he looks back, he's way too close! But once The Hat Man is already in your life and in your home, what can you do?

As I've already preached on and on about, making up your mind on where your loyalties lie between the light and dark—this is the single most important step you can do! No fence sitting allowed and there's no room for self-doubt or doubts in God or Jesus. So apply some Faith generously all over your body and soul, to be sure to help block off some of the advances darkness may attempt to rain down on you.

But say that you know and realize that The Hat Man is just too darn comfortable tromping through your closet or trifling through your home. Even if you get the inkling that something dark may be inspiring negativity in your residence. Heck-even if you are slightly worried about something dark moving into your home or life—there is something you can do about it!

There aren't any rituals or cash needing to be paid to lift a "curse," as so many scamming psychics will tell you. The feeling of needing to attend a church and become a member, just so you can feel the power and legitimacy to have a church behind you—that also isn't "necessary." You aren't even required to contact a pastor or priest to implement the right power of God against darkness.

So now that I've told you all what you don't need, I guess you should know what I'm talking about. First you need to have the three D's: **Desire**, **Dedication** and **Devotion**.

The "Desire" is of course wanting and needing to dispose of and protect against dark elements. "Dedication" is what you'll need to follow through and maintain the process. Then the "Devotion" you must have is to God, there's no other way, so I cannot pretend there is.

Where you will need to apply these three D's, is wherever you call home. Where you live is your place of *being*. Home is where you eat to replenish your energy, bathe to refresh yourself, tumble if you don't watch your step, argue to express yourself, pay bills to maintain your lifestyle, and scoff at the idea of anything you hadn't personally thought of on your own.

We build up and maintain ourselves from the base of our home. So it's no wonder that The Hat Man likes to come and disrupt our solace and foundation there. The advantage on our side when The Hat Man does approach on our homes, is that we aren't what I would consider as being "vulnerable" while at home. Home, for most people, isn't a scary place. Home is familiar, comfortable and may even have a character to it that feels nearly like a friend of the family.

This all means that you have a stronger foothold in your home in any situation, to begin with. Now, if you were out lurking around in a crusty-old, haunted house that wasn't your own, then I would say you might be at a huge disadvantage in the face of evil. But your home is your domain and The Hat Man wasn't invited—or was he?

We already went over all of those possibilities if The Hat Man came due to a known or unknown invitation. In this instance, how he got there is not the issue as long as we are sure we have taken up the Welcome Mat from the front door of your life and home! In fact, I can wait while you go and grab it up and toss it into the dumpster down the street—if you think that's part of the problem.

Okay, you are all done now—I hope.

These are literally the steps that need to be done to get the Bogeyman or Hat Man out and away from your home. It was suggested by a good group of friends of mine to do this method of fully cleaning, clearing and the blessing of one's home. It's helped myself and now countless others who I've shared this process with through the airwaves-worldwide:

Being that I am Christian I make use of and approach what I'm about to share here in a very Christian way. However, I can tell you that my Muslim and Jewish friends have substituted in some of their Faith elements successfully. So the basis is what's important in looking to God to help back you up. Jesus has personally been my rock to break down some evil barriers that I once thought would never break—and He has NEVER failed me nor the others you've read about here!

Items you will need for this blessed task:

1. Natural water, even spring water from a bottle will do.
2. A cross necklace.
3. Other household members.

I realize that numbers one and two are easier to come by than it is to sometimes convince someone you live with to understand the importance of what you are about to do. It is important that everyone who lives in the household participates to some extent, because it is more effective that way. But I have heard of many successful blessings with just one person going through this process, as well:

1. Place the water in the sunlight for at least a couple of hours, to essentially charge it up with one of God's given gifts of Light. NOTE: Make sure you have enough water to bless the entire house and pour the water into a cup or bowl when you are ready to start the blessing.

2. If you own a house and have a basement, start this process in the basement. If you have two stories or more without a basement, start this process on the top floor. If you have a single level home or apartment, start this process at the very furthest point from your front door.

3. Whatever level of the home you are needing to start at, go to the room that is the furthest away from the stairs of the next level or exit.

4. In that furthest room, go to the furthest corner of that room from the door. Leave the door open to the room.

5. Dip your cross into the water and splash it lightly into the sign of the cross. Everyone who is participating in this blessing has to do the exact same thing as each other, meaning you and they are blessing the same things one after the other. It doesn't have to be in the exact same spot, or order, but if a window is blessed by one then it should be blessed by all.

6. As you are making the sign of the cross, say a short prayer out loud of your own making that can sound like or be

this: "God, please protect this family and home and keep all negative things away. In Jesus' Name."

7. Do this same blessing on each window, the walls in between each corner of the room and do the next corner when you reach it.

8. When you reach a closet or cabinet, open it up and bless each individual corner of it. Then close its doors and bless the outside of each door to seal it with the blessing.

9. After you have blessed each corner, window, closet, cupboard and wall, you should only have the door to that room left to bless. This whole time you were blessing the room, the door should be open, so if anything is in there it can leave. So now all of you should exit the room and close the door to it and bless the door itself.

10. As you go down the hall to the next room, bless the corners to the hall and walls.

11. After going room to room for that level, if you started in the basement, now go to the top floor. If you started on the top floor, go to the main floor and repeat steps 3 through 10. Be sure to bless the stairs on your way.

12. The last and final step, once you've blessed everything from the furthest towards the front door of the home, now open the door to your home and say your blessing out loud and ask whatever is there to leave in Jesus' Name. Then close the door and bless it.

13. Sometimes for extra measure, I bless the center of each room after I've done all the corners of a room.

14. I also suggest that the cross necklace that was used in the blessing should actually be worn for at least a couple of days without taking it off. For small kids, maybe hang the cross above their bed.

So there you have it! No hocus-pocus is involved. Just you, a natural element of what God has created, God and Jesus!

Have *no doubts* in your actions and the Power of God and your human potential to tell the unseen to take a hike! These things hide under the cover of darkness or in crevasses-for a reason. It'd be a whole other game if these things knocked on the door, introduced themselves and how they had ill-will towards you and your family. That'd sound almost like a formal invitation to a duel, because you surely wouldn't let things go down without a fight to ensue!

Now, this protection can and will hold. But there are times that something may get stuck on the shoe of someone visiting that might stick to the rug and transform into something big and gummy. No fear, because you can just do the blessing again! Booster shots to up the immunity of your home is always recommended anyways!

The transformation that happens to people after they take the responsibility of blessing their own homes, is tremendous! Think about it, you've visited every corner of your home and checked it for paranormal bugs and exterminated them! You've done the work yourself and I've found that doing so, makes the blessing take more effect than having someone else do the blessing.

Though well-intentioned psychics and mediums, priests, pastors and neighbors with one hand on sage and the other on a crystal—truly aim for the best outcome—sometimes that doesn't happen. To me, it's kind of an odd thing to make use of someone else's Faith to take care of my home and protect my own soul. It's like having someone reach to scratch your back when they don't know where you itch. It's like having someone brush your teeth for you because you forgot to do it. It's like someone doing your homework when it's actually you who has to pass the test.

Do you see how these substitute blessers of your home might fail if the real problems aren't addressed by the one who needs to deal with them?

I'm not saying guidance isn't needed and help isn't' welcomed, but the legwork has to be done from the shingles of the home to the basement of your soul. Shortcuts are exactly that, a short and temporary route to a remedy. But we all know how knockoffs aren't as good as the real thing. The blessing is the easy part and the clearing up of one's soul doesn't have to be thought of as being such a horribly difficult process, either.

Just start somewhere and don't stop until you are satisfied with where you are at. But if you are still worried you haven't hit the mark with your soul level and Faith, you have to know that I already know that people worry about this. I couldn't just tickle the edges of darkness without lifting up the lighter stuff in my writings, of course.

Writing on such gloomy topics has to have a balance, so as mentioned before, I wrote a couple of books on Faith—The Other "F" Word." In my mind, a balance needed to be created even in putting this dark book out!

It's so terribly important that you get your Faith right that I'm going to repeat myself again about some of the tools I put together that I pray will help:

1. For young readers (7 and up) and for anyone who likes to laugh, at 238 pages with over 180 comics I think this will help reach some goals on the Faith path for anyone: *Diary Blog of the Fickle Finders: Investigates (Faith)—The Other "F" Word.* If you or your kids like the *Diary of a Wimpy Kid*

books (dare I say-I've heard back from readers compare it as being just as much fun to read) then I think you will love this series nearly as much!

2. For the rest of us who like to laugh and be sort of practical on what our Faith looks like, smells like, dwells on, gets a kink in its chain, and how to get to the next level: *The Other "F" Word: A Book On Faith in the Real (Funny) World.* With the use of comics also sputtered in this book, I tried to define our Faith lives in a simple format. I think that it's important we can laugh at ourselves and define ourselves while still finding some answers. I aimed to get at the gut of the most stubborn of us in our Faith patterns and holdups, so I hope this book hits its target to make you roll belly up in laughter and submission to your Faith. ☺

I hate to sound like a used car salesman, but kick the tires and get these books on loan at a library or return them to the store after you've read it (okay-I'm not truly suggesting thievery tactics here). Just get started on your journey towards having more confidence in your Faith already, because we need more people on the brightly painted side of the fence!

Faith is SO important, that's why I choose to capitalize it in this book.

I don't have all of the answers to anything. But I can't help but to try and paint the way to a path that I hope works for others, because it truly has worked for me so darn well.

16

HAT MAN MYSTERY:

Is There No End?

There are so many unanswered questions about what is going on with this Hat Man phenomenon. It has apparently been around longer than most people were ever aware, due to the lack of communication. So then it seems that communication is key, because without it and without people sharing what they know about this and other paranormal topics—we all sit in the dark.

To me it feels like the dark side is placing bets on us not to figure them out since we call people "freaks and weirdoes" if they dare to speak out on such things. So people tend to go underground and blog away online in discreet and anonymous fashions in an effort to resolve a little bit here and there. I even know of paranormal radio personalities who have their own shows who choose to use another name just to protect them or their family's reputation! So don't think that all of us who step forward are really using ourselves fully as an example on what to do in the paranormal world.

But you can bet I'm using my real name here. I told my dad I would be sure to keep his last name shining on the front cover of all my books since he didn't have any sons (he wasn't very keen to the idea at first—but he's accepted that fact now—I mean about using my real name, not about having a son)! ☺

I choose to be who I am and come as I am in the paranormal sense and let people judge as they wish. I know what I know and since I can't drag you all with me on my odd journeys, the best I can do is split my gut open down the middle and pour out its contents. If you get a stick and poke around in it, you just might find a jewel or two that might even cling to your own ribs!

That was sort of a gross analogy, huh?

But I urge people to come together on this and other extraordinary topics so we can help each other out. Something has been playing tag with our souls, secretly whispering, "You're it!" All of this without so much as a word being spoken about it. How disturbing is that? Then we leave people alone in that reality of experiencing the sinister touch of the freaking devil—of all things?! How cruel!

The Hat Man is nothing that a person should take on alone.

If that witness to seeing him is not able to talk to someone, reach out in some way, heck—then reach out to me! Vent what's going on, get involved in posting your story online to help make others aware of the threat of this thing. Do something, do or say anything and do it well without the worry of what others might think. If you are worried about that, worry more about what God would think and how proud He would be that you took a stance against evil harming others.

Get this, I was done writing this book and I got to supervise a new occupational therapy student for the day. In talking with another colleague about my extracurricular activities involving Shadow People, my student spoke up as if to know all about them! I let her know that it was me who gave this horrible phenomenon their name and spread it out to the masses. She then told me of a horrific encounter she had when she was only four years old:

"I was playing with a bobby pin and looking at an electrical outlet right next to me along the wall. I was a little kid, but I knew I wasn't supposed to poke anything in those holes. Then I heard in my head in a deep, guttural voice say, "Go ahead—stick it in!"

"When I looked up, there was this huge man in a fedora type hat, all in black, with no face! He was completely shadowed and he scared me to death! I was actually thinking about putting the bobby pin in the wall socket, but he got me so scared that I ran to tell my parents!"

I swear to you that I am not hunting people down to see who has experienced The Hat Man or Shadow People. It's just THAT common that this Hat Man is hunting that many people for their souls. I don't have to go far before hearing of him and his acts. If I randomly threw an egg into a small crowd, I'm sure it would splatter bits onto at least three people who have experienced The Hat Man or Shadow People.

But this story of encouraging childhood suicide makes you wonder how many children listened to this sort of encouragement from this dark predator—doesn't it?! Then as The Hat Man collected their young souls, what did he do with them and what kind of horror did they endure? Do you feel the urgency in what I'm sharing here even more now?

For those of you who truly still feel alone in all of this, know that you can stand on your own two feet and remain strong in the face of such evil. The only way that is possible is by having goodness back you up, ying gets yang, dark hates light and the devil hates Jesus. So what else is there to say, but for people to take to finding the Light in their lives with God written all over it!

The mystery will continue, but individual battles can and will be won. I have a saying that I usually apply to other situations, but I think I can adapt it appropriately here:

"The day that I can understand evil fully, then I'm just as evil as the evil."

In other words, the day that I will know all of the answers to such a horrible thing as The Hat Man, then I must be WAY too close to him. We can all as researchers and authors try pointing the way to answers about why something exists as it does and its purpose. But we may miss the mark because our ego makes us blind to what's truly important, we haven't experienced things personally, or because we want to be the ones to discover something and be known for it. For example, often times people and researchers like to focus on odd little details of what Jesus looked like, dressed like and other bits that REALLY don't matter in the end. Because it all only distracts away from the bigger picture of who Jesus is and what He's done and continues to do in protecting us from bad things like The Hat Man!

In a roundabout way, I get a similar sense about The Hat Man and other evil garbage.

If I get down on my knees to scrape up some dirt so I can figure out why dirt is able to cause bad stains in my jeans-that just might distract me from what I should really be looking at. I know the dirt is there, so I've just got to find the right detergent to get the crap out of the knee stains I have now because I was kneeling in it! I was too caught up in trying to find answers while ignoring the main problem of getting on my knees in the first place!

Hold-on, was that confusing?

If we get too close, I think we risk the chance of getting dirty in the process when that risk isn't even necessary. So allow me to do some fine reporting from a helicopter, flying overhead as I track the villain from a distance on where he's going so you can avoid the certain traffic jam to come on your spiritual highway.

NOTE: I swear I don't plan out these analogies; they just come out of nowhere and shock me myself. But I do like to think they get inspired to be written by the greatest orator and analogy creator of all time: Jesus! Jesus once told me He'd give me the words to put out there when needed. Though I am far from being a saint of any sort, but I sure take comfort in knowing that He's near and most certainly inspiring. I hope and pray that all of you keep steady in your gaze towards Him and enlightenment.

There's so much in this world that remains a mystery, but we do know that evil is well known among us. We know the feel of it, agony of it, and success of it, but one thing we don't know is the defeat of it! Don't you think it's about time that we know the taste of victory in defeating evil for all of us? I think that it's time we came to the challenge that's already been smacking us in the back of our heads while we weren't looking and head-butt it back into the hole it crawled out of.

So, let's get to it now then—shall we?

This book isn't over just because I stopped writing in it. So take hold of the solution and move on to the next topic of Faith so we can all smile again knowing that doom and gloom isn't the end of this story. To quote one of my favorite Dr. Seuss books, while in thinking what's possible when you've got God on your side, "Oh, the places you'll go!"

Blessed Journeys and God's Protection to You All,
In Jesus' Name ☺
~Heidi

About the Author

Heidi Hollis is a unique voice in this paranormally-challenged world of ours. From angels to aliens and for over 20 years, Hollis has tackled mysterious topics from a very young age. She is an advocate for bringing extraordinary topics to a comfortable level where they can be spoken of openly and without shame— even with a hint of humor! She has written for various publications and is sought worldwide for her levelheaded advice and research into many of the world's most intriguing phenomena.

Hollis is also the radio talk show host of the lively paranormal broadcasts, "Heidi Hollis-The Outlander" and co-host of "The Kevin Cook Show," both currently on Inception Radio Network. In addition, Hollis is a practicing Occupational Therapist (OTR/L), columnist, lecturer, movie producer and is an accomplished cartoonist as seen in her new graphic novel series, "Diary Blog of the Fickle Finders." This book series appeals to all ages and will cover all of the same topics Hollis addresses from angels to aliens—but with hundreds of comics meant to hit the funny bone and the brain at the same time!

For up-to-date information about Heidi Hollis and her many events and projects to come, please visit:

Websites:
www.HeidiHollis.com
www.UFO2U.com
www.FickleFinders.com
www.ParanormalPledge.com
www.Facebook.com/1HeidiHollis
www.YouTube.com/HeidiHollis
www.Twitter.com/1HeidiHollis

Online Groups:
1. www.Facebook.com/groups/ParanormalPledge/
2. https://www.facebook.com/groups/ShadowPeopleHatMan/
3. http://tech.groups.yahoo.com/group/UFO2U/
4. https://www.facebook.com/FickleFinders
5. https://www.facebook.com/HeidiHollis.FanPage

CPSIA information can be obtained
at www.ICGtesting.com
Printed in the USA
BVHW072350010323
659482BV00004B/74